I0519451

GOD HAS CHOSEN ME

MY LIFE WITH CHRIST

Morales Gaintilus

Copyright © 2024 by Morales Saintilus

ISBN: 978-1-963917-04-8 (hardbook)
ISBN: 978-1-963917-03-1 (softcover)
ISBN: 978-1-963917-05-5 (ebook)
Library of Congress Control Number: 2024905173

All rights reserved. No part of this book may be reproduced or transmitted in any form or by any means, electronic or mechanical, including photocopying, recording, or by any information storage and retrieval system without express written permission from the author, except in the case of brief quotations embodied in critical reviews and certain other noncommercial uses permitted by copyright law.

Printed in the United States of America.

Contents

PROLOGUE · i

DEDICATION · iv

ACKNOWLEDGMENTS · v

CHAPTER 1 · 6
Revelations and Confirmations

CHAPTER 2 · 11
The Lord Revealed Himself To Abraham

CHAPTER 3 · 18
The Lord Revealed Himself To Isaac and Jacob

CHAPTER 4 · 26
The Lord Revealed Himself To Moses

CHAPTER 5 · 32
The Furious Antagonism Between Satan, The Great
Tempter and Jesus, The Founder of the New Covenant

CHAPTER 6 · 37
The Lord Revealed Himself To Philip

CHAPTER 7 • 39

    The Lord Revealed Himself To Saul of Tarsus and Ananias

CHAPTER 8 • 43

    The Lord Revealed Himself To Cornelius and Peter

CHAPTER 9 • 49

    The Origin and Growth of My Life in Christ

CHAPTER 10 • 63

    My Mentor

CHAPTER 11 • 67

    Divine Interventions

CHAPTER 12 • 89

    Tributes and Recognition

Prologue

Over fifty years ago, or at the age of eleven, a man in white clothes appeared to me in a dream and said: **"The Lord has chosen you among your people and you belong to him."**

To confirm his call in my life, he swarmed me with revelations and divine interventions. He then granted me great deliverances in the face of great dangers.

The boulevard of Cap-Haitian was considered as a center of study for all concerned students, from elementary to philosophy (Advanced 12th Grade)). May 4, 1974, three o'clock in the afternoon, while I was studying, a man about five feet seven inches tall, with his suitcase in hand, approached me and said to me: **"You will become a great servant of God; but prepare yourself for a merciless war with Satan and his emissaries. They will rally all their allies to make sure that your name is forever erased on the face of the earth. You will be struck, repeatedly, by great distresses; but his plan will not be carried out, for the Lord will come to your rescue"**, and he was gone.

I was so serious and attached to my studies that I felt really distracted by this unexpected interlocutor; but, out of politeness, I listened to him. It has already been thirty three years, while I was writing this book. I remember that moment, as if this man were still standing in front of me. I paid little attention to what he had to say and, after he left, I continued my studies with more concentration.

In addition, these kinds of men are titled to prophets of doom, tellers of good adventures, mediums or evil angels. Today I realized that everything he predicted was fulfilled to the letter. Was that man an angel? God only knows. The Holy Spirit has encouraged me to take and keep accurate records of almost every event in my life, whether they were happy or unhappy.

However, I never pretended to write a book. I always thought at my young age that the profession of writer was only reserved for geniuses. But after a spectacular miracle which the Lord has accomplished in my life, a miracle which has brought before me all the graces and deliverances which the Lord has granted me in sharing, I decided to write a book whose pages would contain the wonders of the Almighty in my life.

I never had the blessing of reaching this beautiful dream that haunted me, almost nine years ago.

After these long years, the Lord has sealed it with his own seal, and has proceeded to its realization. I repeat: I always thought that the profession of writer or christian writer would never be realized in my life for two reasons: first, in the environment where I grew up, I observed that a small percentage among the most fortunate had the chance to attend school; and a fraction of that rate almost negligible, had the fortune to attain a higher education; second, my parents were hard labourers, just to make sure that we, their children, had not gone hungry. However, they did not think of offering us a higher education, due to their economic situation and the attitude of my environment who thought that higher education and even ordinary education were not necessary. But the Lord simultaneously proved that my deduction was true and the opposite was also true. My deduction was true, in that, more than forty years after the first revelation and all the revelations that followed, it had never crossed my mind even a simple conjecture to write a book. The opposite was also the case, since the Lord miraculously allowed me to have access to higher education and opened to me the locks of heavens and placed in me an inexhaustible source of inspiration which bound me to tell the wonders of the Lord through literature, lecture, teaching and preaching the rest of my life.

So therefore, this work that I present to you today, dear readers, and the works to appear whose number I do not yet know, will not be of my decision or my intelligence, but, that of the supreme God whose abode is in the highest heavens and that the eyes dominate on the earth and heaven and also penetrate the depths of the heart of man or of every human being, living on the face of the earth.

May the Lord, dear reader, animate you with humility and obedience to read this work with sustained attention! May he help you find in it a source of inspiration and passion that will lead you to the beatitudes of an admirable God who has no bias: rich or poor; learned or ignorant; Jew or pagan.

Friday, May 27, 2005.
MORALES SAINTILUS
Revised On December 18, 2023

DEDICATIONS

I dedicate this work to my deceased parents: Fadeus and Talicia Saintilus; my distinguished wife, Margalie Saintilus; my only beloved son, Doctor Molain Saintilus, his wonderful wife, Jeanina Saintilus and their children, also my adorable grandchildren, Angelica Saintilus and Sage Saintilus; to my sister and brother-in-law: Adelicia and Hortencius Toussaint; to my four cousins who have done me a lot of good, from my tender adolescence to my adulthood: Siliane Bissainthe, Eliette Georges, Wilson Saintilus and Alexis Francis.

To my nephews and nieces: Sem Toussaint, Roniel Toussaint, Ernsie Dénoschamp, Milouse Saintilus, Arnaud Guerrier, Arniel Guerrier, Renaud Guerrier, Verose Rock, Anne-Marie Rock, Camanio Rock and and Dadesky Rock.

To my dear cousins whom I grew with and that I loved deeply: Marie Violeine Casseus, Rinice Marie Saintilus, Wilfrid Saintilus, Henry Saintilus, Henri-Claude Saintilus, George Saintilus, Marie Renande Saintilus.

ACKNOWLEDMENTS

My thanks go first to my God who, in my indignity chose me to make his glory shine, and to my admirable wife, Margalie Saintilus who crossed, with me, climbs and valleys to respond to the divine call that the Lord has made to us.

To my deceased parents: Fadéus and Talicia Saintilus for whom, my admiration and my filial love still remain alive in my heart being even in the grave.

To my beloved sister Adelucia Toussaint and her husband Hortencius Toussaint.

CHAPTER ONE
Revelations & Confirmations

Friday May 27, 2005, around ten o'clock in the morning, I was blessed to find myself in the middle of a sunny nature, where the morning breeze, like that of noon time, caressed the green leaves of an alley of ornamental trees. They moved in such a harmonious rhythm that every christian heart should have thought of the majesty, the wisdom, and the holiness of a God so great, so marvelous, so infinite. And while I was contemplating his magnificent wonders, I quickly recognized my smallness and I began to exalt with David in **Psalm 8:3-4:**

> *"When I consider your heavens, the work of your fingers,*
> *The moon and the stars, which you have ordained,*
> *What is man that you are mindful of him,*
> *And the son of man that you visit him?*
> *For you have made him a little lower than the angels,*
> *And you have crowned him with glory and honor."*

And, as filled with the Holy Spirit, I celebrated, I exalted, I magnified the Lord with tears of wonder. At the time of this holy and happy manifestation, I felt in jubilation, and I heard a voice coming from nowhere, saying: **"Go; write down and declare all that you have seen and heard and strengthen my people"**.

I fell on my knees and I said to my God: Yes Lord, I recognize that it is you. Our life is an open book before you, and you know us better than we do. You have placed with your indescribable science, each cell that makes up our being. How many of our thoughts have escaped us; have they plunged into the annals of oblivion! But you, you can list them one by one without omitting an iota! You can tell us what will happen a second or a million years later, without saving a moment of repentance. This is why I want to obey you without questioning and wait for your miracle without a doubt.

In this moment of perfect reverence, I felt in ecstasy. I went to sit down, perplexed and confused to pray. Immediately after prayer, the title of this book was inspired to me: **MY LIFE WITH CHRIST**. When I was about to finish this writing, someone had appeared to me in vision, sat at my right side, passed his hand around my stroke, said to me, like a tender and trusted friend: listen, "Call not your book: **MY LIFE WITH CHRIST, but rather: CHRIST HAS CHOSEN ME**".

When I woke up, I was in a state of fullness and I said: Lord, God, it is obvious that you have placed your Spirit in me to fulfill your will. That same Friday, May 27, 2005, I had to go to Lebanon Baptist Camp, New Jersey. We were leaving around six in the evening for a weekend family retreat organized by **THE ALLIANCE OF THE HAITIAN BAPTIST CHURCHES OF THE UNITED STATES** where I was then president.

This alliance brought together more than forty churches, scattered in about twelve states or regions of the United States, with the aim of uniting them, strengthening them and forming some kind of solidarity in the community of Haitian Christians.

This part of New Jersey called Lebanon is a hidden place. There, there is little traffic and pollution; there, we breathe a better and purer air than elsewhere. It is a large piece of land, embellished with green lawn, trees whose foliage did not seem to wilt. There, whoever seeks God will have the blessing of marveling at the richness of his glory. He will have the joy of meeting this God whom Moses calls: "Magnificent in holiness";

that Hannah calls: "My strength"; that Zechariah calls: "God Faithful"; that Morales calls; "Infinite Wisdom."

Since I had come into direct contact with this perfect God, my mind could not move away from his presence. Inside my dormitory, I meditated on the richness of his goodness. Outside, my soul was captured by the green lawn, the soft murmur of the trees' leaves where the morning breeze, cuddled cautiously; by small repeated flights of replaying birds. At this moment, this ground and air armies mixed their voice with mine to sing eternally: **"Glory, glory to the Lord."**

After this spiritual experience, like a foreign being coming from a foreign country, from the country of eternal glory, I approached the cafeteria for breakfast. It was on May 29, 2005, around eight in the morning. There, a brother greeted me with a warm smile and said to me: "Have a seat, Sir, Mr. President. It is for you that I have reserved this seat". I appreciated it with a big thank you and I added: God bless you, my brother.

For me, it was the first time I met this brother. I asked him: have you ever met me before, my brother? "Most certainly, pastor," he warmly replied! He continued, "You have preached for us in our church, and we have been richly blessed."

"Pastor Morales", he added, "I would like to tell you something". Of course! I kindly replied. So let's sit down, I told him. We sat down and he said to me: "I would like to ask someone to write a book about you and Sister Morales, your beloved wife and bring me the result.

For, it didn't take me long to observe the two of you and determine that your life is an example of Christian love, humility and talent. Many have borne witness to it". I was on the slope to exclaim, very loudly, like a madman: o God, of infinite wisdom! But, I restrained myself and hastened to say: thank you! And I continued: well, my brother, all the glory is to the Lord! This is how God wants us to live for him on earth.

Providentially, this someone he was looking to write this book was, indeed, I, your servant, who was chosen to write this book by the infinitely wise, holy and just God, two days before this brother, on May 27, 2005.

Without saying another word to this beloved brother, except to ask: please give me a minute, and I will get back to you right away. I hastened outside to exclaim: blessed your name, the Lord, my God! It is certain it was you who sent this brother to convince me of your revelation: that of testifying, in writing, "All that I saw and heard, and strengthen your people". And when I was back to ask this brother his name and the church he belonged to, he was gone.

I searched for the rest of the day to gather accurate information from him and his church for inclusion in this work, as proof of the vocation to which "God thrice holy" has called me. No answer!

I conducted several other investigations in our churches, I never found him. I quite simply concluded that God was using him to confirm the call he has made to me, or for sure, I was visited by the angel of the Lord.

I was looking for some kind of evidence, support and witness, but the Lord does not need any of this. What he did, he did and everyone will know that he did it. Whether it was a man or an angel, his mission was to carry out the divine order and that was it.

This divine revelation and confirmation, I am convinced, will not be a surprise or questioned by those who are attached to the study of the bible, the words of God, since the Lord was revealed himself in the same way:

A) In the Old Testament to:
a) Abraham
b) Isaac
c) Jacob
d) Moses

B) In the New Testament, after the antagonism between Jesus Christ and Satan to:

a) Philip and the Ethiopian Minister
b) Saul of Tarsus and Ananias
c) Peter and Cornelius
Just to name a few of the best known.

CHAPTER TWO
The Lord Revealed Himself To Abraham

So let's start this epic with Abraham. The latter is history and this history must begin its narrative with the countries of his origin which present real confusion for many. May the Holy Spirit enlighten me, to clarify this confusion, before sketching this marvelous story of the life of Abraham and his close relationship with the true God.

The names of the countries which are attached to his childhood until adulthood, seventy five years, to be exact, are the following: Shinar, Babel or Tower of Babel, Babylonia, Babylon, Chaldea, Ur and Mesopotamia.

Let's identify them one by one:
1. Shinar or Sinead was a plain, a country or an extent of country inside which were: Babel, Babylon, Babylonia, Chaldea and Ur.

Babel or Tower of Babel was a city of this plain. Everyone knows the story of this tower where Noah's descendants had decided to compete with their Creator, or to use biblical language, "to revolt against God", by building a tower that would touch the sky, in order to establish a permanent kingdom. What was contrary to God's order: "be fertile, multiply, fill the earth" (Genesis 1:28)

Their plan which resulted from the disobedience of man to the order of the Creator was reduced to nothing, when the Almighty confused their language. This is how they were scattered over the face of the earth, and the plan of the omniscient God was accomplished.

Babylonia. Babylonia was a country in western Asia. It was in turn called: Shinar, country of the Chaldeans and had become an empire: the Babylonian empire.

Babylon. Babylon was the capital of the Babylonian Empire. It was also there that Noah's descendants undertook the construction of the tower of Babel where Nimrod, the grandson of Cush, was the grand monarch or the powerful emperor.

Chaldea. Chaldea was originally located south of Babylonia. But, it had later become so powerful that it usurped the name of Babylonia.

Ur. Ur, was the country of the birthplace of Abraham, was a large and prosperous city of Chaldea and was also, later called: Babylonia.

Mesopotamia. Mesopotamia was a country located between the river of the tiger and that of the Euphrates. It was located on the edge of Babylonia. Later, it extended into the interior of Babylonia so that Stephen located the Ur of Chaldea in Mesopotamia (Acts 7: 2).

Let us remember that Ur, in Chaldea, was the country of the birthplace of Abraham. Chaldea was a city in Babylonia which was itself the cradle of idolatry. The false gods swarmed there. The whole country indulged in the worship of these false gods, these imaginary gods.

Apart from these false gods, represented by the pantheon of the Babylonian empire, pantheon which included gods of the world: astral deities, gods of nature, national gods. This empire also embraced these primitive religions, such as: fetishism, worship of fetishes which were objects and animals to which magical or beneficial properties were attributed; animism, a form of religion which has attributed a soul to animals, phenomena and natural objects; totetism which was a religion or social organization based on the totem, represented by an animal, a plant, or an object considered as protectors of an individual or as mythical ancestors, representing a social group in relation to other social groups to other groups of the same company. The totem is also the carved or painted representation of this animal, this plant or this object.

Born and raised in a country mired in these pernicious practices, Abraham refused to participate, and contrary to his fellow citizens, he chose a different and unique religion: the worship of the one true God.

In truth, before Abraham's call, the Bible gave no explanation for his choice of religion. I had no information; you had none, of course, either. But, the almighty God has already detected all the movements in Abraham's heart who rejected all the other gods, to choose the only true God. All these deductions are updated, after Abraham's vocation.

The Lord revealed himself to Abraham and said to him,

"Get out of your country,
From your family
And from your father's house,
To a land that I will show you.
² I will make you a great nation;
I will bless you
And make your name great;
And you shall be a blessing.

I will bless those who bless you,
And I will curse him who curses you;
And in you all the families of the earth shall be blessed."
Genesis 12: 1-3

From my deduction, and I believe I am inspired by the Holy Spirit; a double motivation prompted the Lord to order Abraham to leave his homeland:

1. It would be almost impossible for Abraham to worship a foreign god in a country where everyone embraced the same pernicious practices: the worship of imaginary gods and all that is similar.

2. The Lord wanted to test Abraham's faith and obedience before granting him the official title that no other human has ever held on earth: "father of faith". Yes, the God he chose ordered him to leave behind him: his career, his parents, his friends and all that was dear to him, to embark on a precarious journey and uncertain destination. But, how did Abraham begin to accept an order that seemed so authoritative and vague, without any resistance or debate? Indeed, he blindly believed in the fidelity and the omnipotence of the God whom he newly chose.

Who can probe the wisdom of the Lord? Have we forgotten that he is the omniscient God? However, he opened my mind to detect two main reasons for his actions concerning Abraham's vocation. Before updating these two divine actions revealed, let us first turn to his call or his vocation.

When the Lord called him, he did not say: go from your land and take your parents with you or some members of your family? However, he took with him his father Terach and his nephew Lot. I do not mention Sara, his wife, in marriage, according to God himself, "man and woman become one flesh". And, moreover, Sara shared her husband's faith and was entirely subject to his will.

Was it God's will that Abraham took his father Terach and his nephew Lot with him? My intuition or spiritual inspiration forced me to say no. And, the next two actions of the Lord will prove me right. Let us therefore see the actions of the great wisdom of the Lord that he revealed to me against Abraham's decisions, those to take with him: Terach, his father and Lot, his nephew.

TWO ACTIONS OF THE LORD AGAINST ABRAHAM'S DECISIONS

Why did Abraham stop at Charan with his family where they stayed for so long? Because the Lord did not want Terach to go with him to Canaan.

The main reason was revealed to Joshua by the Lord himself. Joshua said to the people of Israel: "thus, says the Lord, the God of Israel: your fathers, that is to say, the ancestors of Abraham: Terach, his father and his descendants, formerly dwelt in the other side of the Jordan, which means, Ur, in Chaldee, and they served other gods" (**Read Joshua 24: 2**)

FIRST- The Lord therefore prevented Terach from going with him to Canaan because he did not know his God, but the gods of his fathers, the false gods, the imaginary gods.

So therefore, to avoid a confusion of religion in the house of Abraham, or, in order not to interfere in his decisions to serve him freely, the Lord eliminated Terach being in Charan. In a word, Terach was dead in Charan.

The Lord's second action is manifested in the separation of Lot from Abraham (**Read Genesis 13: 2-12**). This text clearly explains that Abraham allowed himself to be led by the Spirit of God, and Lot, the spirit of the flesh. Lot loved the Lord, but his heart was more attached to the things of the century. There was a quarrel between Abraham shepherds and those of Lot, because of the vastness of their flocks.

So Abram said to Lot: "Please let there be no strife between you and me, and between my herdsmen and your herdsmen; for we are brethren. Is not the whole land before you? Separate yourself from me. If you take the left, then I will go to the right; or, if you go to the right, then I will go to the left."

And Lot lifted his eyes and saw all the plain of Jordan, that it was well watered everywhere (before the LORD destroyed Sodom and Gomorrah) like the garden of the LORD, like the land of Egypt as you go toward Zoar. Then Lot chose for himself all the plain of Jordan, and Lot journeyed east. And they separated from each other. Abram dwelt in the land of Canaan, and Lot dwelt in the cities of the plain and pitched *his* tent even as far as Sodom. But the men of Sodom was exceedingly wicked and sinful against the LORD. **(Genesis 13:8-12)**

Before separating these two men, Abraham and Lot, so as never to reunite as a family, the Lord exposed the incompatible differences between the two:

a) Abraham was a champion of peace: "Let there be no dispute between me and you; between my shepherds and your shepherds. For we are brethren".

b) An altruist, in the deepest sense of the term. Since he was like a father to Lot, he could take responsibility for all of the herds. On the contrary, it helped him to be very wealthy. His selflessness had spread even further, in plain sight, when he said to Lot: "Isn't the country before you?

If you go to the right, I will go to the left; if you go to the left, I go to the right". By this fact, Abraham ceded his right of uncle or father to Lot, offering him the opportunity to choose first.

There is no doubt that Abraham can only be a man tamed by the Spirit of God or a man after the heart of God, while Lot was driven by envy and lust. So his heart was more attached to earthly things, rather than God.

c) Abraham let him choose first. He took advantage of this unexpected opportunity to choose the most fertile part of the country. The bible says: Lot looked up and saw all the part of the Jordan, which was entirely watered. I guess he certainly said in his heart: this is where milk and honey flow.

In his envious heart, he crossed the border of paradise to advance towards Sodom and Gomorrha who were, at the time, earthly hell, awaiting the manifestation of the wrath of God. For their inhabitants were great sinners against the Lord. This is how the Lord did the second action, drawing Lot away from Abraham with an endless goodbye. It was then and only then that the Lord was ready to fulfill his promises in Abraham's life; specially, the promise to give him the Promised Land which was Canaan.

REASONS FOR ABRAHAM'S VOCATION

The Lord has now revealed the reasons for the choice of Abraham as his friend and his title of 'father of faith', or 'father of all believers'.

1. Unlike his fellow citizens, Abraham chose a different and unique religion: the worship of the one true almighty God (Read Genesis 17; 1); the eternal God; the God very high, Master of heaven and earth; the just, righteous God who exercises righteousness over all the earth (**Genesis 18:25**).

   Abraham believed in the Lord. This is why God has strengthened his faith to never give up on him, revealing himself to him many times. (**Genesis 12: 1-3, 7; 13: 14-18; 15; 17: 1-21, etc.**)

2. Apart from other exercises of faith, God raised up one which was the supreme test, by which Abraham was to give full measure of his faith: the call to the sacrifice of Isaac, his only and spoiled son (read Genesis 22). The author of the epistle to the Hebrews did not fail to appreciate also, this sublime action of Abraham (**Hebrews 11: 17-18**).

CHAPTER THREE
GOD REVEALED HIMSELF TO ISAAC & JACOB

Isaac was Abraham's legitimate son, and he was called the son of the promise, for the Lord promised him to Abraham and gave him according to his promise. Abraham and Jacob led a more active life than Isaac in action and in contact with God. But, God has proved that does not make any difference. For he formed a chain in three meshes on which were inscribed: "God of Abraham, Isaac and Jacob". The simple signs of distinction between them are explained by the fact that Isaac was a little softer and more peaceful; that he became very thoughtful and lonely at the death of his mother who loved him unconditionally and that he loved and cherished tenderly. This void was filled when he married Rebecca. (**Genesis 24: 63-67**)

Besides the famine that struck Canaan in the time of Abraham, a second famine struck this country again at the time of Isaac. And the latter sought refuge with Abimelec, king of the Philistines, with the intention of going to Egypt where there was, certainly, a greater abundance of provisions. But the Lord revealed himself to Isaac to test his faith by ordering him not to go to Egypt and to stay in Gerar, the land of the Philistines. Isaac blindly obeyed to his God (**Genesis 26: 1-6**):

"There was a famine in the land, besides the first famine that was in the days of Abraham. And Isaac went to Abimelech king of the Philistines, in Gerar."

Then the Lord appeared to him and said: "Do not go down to Egypt; live in the land of which I shall tell you. Dwell in this land, and I will be with you and bless you; for to you and your descendants I give all these lands, and I will perform the oath which I swore to Abraham your father. And I will make your descendants multiply as the stars of heaven; I will give to your descendants all these lands; and in your seed all the nations of the earth shall be blessed; because Abraham obeyed My voice and kept My charge, My commandments, My statutes, and My laws."

So Isaac dwelt in Gerar.

The Lord is ready to open the floodgates of heaven for all who hear his voice and obey him. Since Isaac blindly obeyed the command of his God, he showered him with such great blessings at Gerar that its inhabitants felt jealous against him (**Genesis 26:12**).

The Lord revealed himself to Isaac on still more satisfactory terms. This time he passed on to him the promises he made to Abraham, his father (**Genesis 26: 31**).

GOD REVEALED HIMSELF TO JACOB

Jacob was the son of Isaac and Rebecca, also, Esau's twin brother. He was born immediately after Esau. For this, he was considered the cadet and Esau, the groin (**Genesis 25: 21-26**). Isaac was sixty years old when his sons were born. The etymology of the name Jacob says that it means: the rascal; cunning. This name also means: God guards and protects. Like his father, Jacob was calm and peaceful in nature (**Genesis 25:27**).

The family was partially divided, in that Isaac preferred Esau and Rebecca pampered Jacob. We should not suppose to ignore that, at the time, there was a birthright in Israel, a special or privileged right, considered as the exclusive property of the first born of a family. The eldest son or first born inherited the rank and the prerogatives from the father. When he died, he became head of the family. He also inherited a double portion of his property. It is also the groin who received, first, the last and most precious of the blessings that the father bestowed on his children at the end of his life.

So let's follow, therefore carefully, the sequence of events:

Rebecca, the twin's mother, I mean, Esau and Jacob, suspecting that Isaac was dying and was ready to offer his last blessings to his sons, the best of which were reserved for Esau, hasted to use a proven ingenuity, worse than that of the pagan, to force Jacob to usurp or steal Esau's blessings. She used an unfair and coarse trick, revealed in Genesis 27: 6. Jacob feared it and refused to collaborate with his mother. (Genesis 27: 11-12). In spite of his irrefutable decisions, he continued to listen to the authority of his mother who eventually convinced him (Genesis 27:13-17).

Certainly Jacob received the desired blessings, but not according to God's plan. From this drama, this reversal of fortune, we learn the following lessons:

a)   Whatever our disposition to obey, to be faithful to God, if we listen to the voice of the tempter or of his emissary, they can easily divert us from his will.

b)   Jacob's reasoning had almost the same weight as those of Adam and Eve, but the three were unsuccessful under the ingenuity of Satan. If we put these two texts in parallel: Genesis 3:1-6 and Genesis 27:1-40, we can immediately notice their similarity in the fact that Satan used the serpent to seduce Eve and Rebecca to seduce his son Jacob.

"Submit yourselves, then, to God. Resist the devil, and he will flee from you". (James 4: 7)

One can resist the devil in prayer and by answering him: It is not only that God said, but what he said is absolutely true. No more discussion about it! In whatever form Satan presents himself, declare that you recognize him and order: depart, Satan! Do not give him any opportunity for conversation.

Establishing a conversation with him is his bait, the great trap he sets up in front of us to lock us in his net. His power can only be tamed by divine providence, consecration to prayer and the fear of God.

God's children do not need to use tricks, subtlety, or obey the voice of Satan to make their dreams come true. Thus, as he did for Jacob, the Lord has already signed the plan of their life; Yahweh has already set up very clear paths for them.

So let's continue with Jacob. Before his birth, the Lord announced that he was going to pass on the birthright to him since in his omniscience, he already indicated that Jacob was going to choose him for his God and Esau, the foreign gods; that Jacob was going to give all importance to spiritual things, while Esau would pay no respect.

Before the twins were born, the Lord said to Rebecca, their mother: **"Two nations are in thy womb, and two people shall separate from thy bowels; one of these people shall be stronger than the other; and the elder shall be subject to the younger"** (Geneses 25:23).

The prophet Malachi and especially the apostle Paul made it even clearer with the following revelations:

a) Malachi 1: 2-3a
"I have loved you, says the Lord. And you say: In what did you love us? Is Esau not Jacob's brother, says the Lord. However, I loved Jacob, and I hated Esau".

b) Romans 9: 11-13
"Even though the children were not yet born and they would have done neither right nor wrong, so that the plan of God's election would subsist, without depending on works, and by the sole will of the caller".

It was said to Rebecca: "The elder will serve the younger"; as it is written:

"I liked Jacob
And I hated Esau".

Many would say that these words are harsh and rigid; they don't seem to be of God. They come exactly from God. They mean: Jacob will choose me and Esau will reject me, and that's it! For the Lord has said of his own lips, this might be in **Isaiah 46: 9-10:** "Remember the former things of old: for I am God, and there is none else; I am God, and there is none like me.

Declaring the end from the beginning, and from ancient times, the things that are not yet done, saying, my counsel shall stand, and I will do all my pleasure. Esau proved God's omniscience when he sold his birthright to Jacob. This scenario is reported in **Genesis 25: 29-34:** and Jacob sod pottage: "And Esau came from the field, and he was faint": "And Esau said to Jacob, Feed me, I pray thee, with that same red pottage; for I am faint: therefore was his name called Edom".

And Jacob said; "Sell me this day thy birthright".

And Esau said,"Behold, I am at the point to die: and what profit shall this birthright do to me?"

And Jacob said, "Swear to me this day"; and he swore unto him: and he sold his birthright unto Jacob.

Then Jacob gave Esau bread and pottage of lentils; and he did eat and drink, and rose up, and went his way: thus Esau despised his birthright.

The birthright, at the time, in Israel, was something sacred, precious and a direct blessing from the Lord. But, Esau trampled it under foot. As the Lord God foretold and that's it.

Esau and Jacob's descendants formed two nations; two different peoples. While Esau's descendants rejected the Lord to establish a heathen nation, called: the Edomites, having their own gods; Jacob's descendants or the people of Israel, on the contrary, adopted the God of their fathers, the God of Abraham, Isaac and Jacob; the supreme God; the only true God.

The Edomites and the Israelites became staunch enemies when the king of Edom, at the exit of the Israelite from the land of Egypt, refused to let them cross into their territory to go to Canaan, and warned them with threat; if they insisted, they would be attacked with rage and without mercy.

On the other hand, since Esau decided to kill Jacob, Rebecca, their mother, arranged to send him to Charan, his native country and she used the same carnal ingenuity again, to bring Isaac to agree with her. Yet the Lord did not abandon Jacob. For, on the way, he made his first and dazzling revelation to encourage and strengthen him. (**Read Genesis 28:10-22**)

As soon as he arrived in Charan, Jacob miraculously met Rachelle, his future wife. But, he paid dearly for his malicious deal with his mother which led him to usurp Esau's blessings, instead of waiting for the fulfillment of God's plan in his life. What he did to Esau, Laban, his future father-in-law, reciprocated. He made him work for seven years before giving him Rachel's hand, which was legal in his time. So, after these years of hard work, he hoped, with outpouring of heart, to unite with his legitimate wife. But Laban, Rachel's father, tricked him into giving him Leah's hand, his older daughter.

Now he has once again required Jacob to work another seven years before giving him the hand of the one whom his heart loved. And, as punishment for her malice, Rebecca, Jacob's mother lost sight of him, her son whom she deeply pampered, and that, until her death.

What an unbearable pain! What a sorrow! Who knows if it were not the depression of Jacob's absence that led her to the grave?

All this, I suppose, was the result of a personal decision, without the participation of the God who has, in his hand: the past, the present, and the future.

The lesson that can be drawn from this drama is that, whatever the complexity of a situation, the christian must solely lean on the unfathomable mercy of Almighty God. Far from God's counsel, without his infallible guidance, even when we had set our feet on heaven, hell would have made its appearance.

At the center of all these confusions and despite his sins committed against God, the compassionate God never abandoned Jacob. And, despite all the apparent weaknesses in his life, his heart belongs only to his God. He chose his father's God as the only true God. Therefore, being even in Laban, after having paid for his sins, and sincerely repented, the Lord showered him with great blessings. This even aroused the jealousy of his brothers-in-law.

Seeing him in danger, the Lord revealed himself again to Jacob and said to him, *"Return to the land of your fathers, and to your birthplace, and I will be with you."* (**Genesis 31:1-3**)

The Lord revealed himself again to Jacob (**Genesis 32:24-30**). In this revelation, the Lord simulated that Jacob wrestled with him and won the victory. Indeed, no warrior, no power over the earth and in heavens, could and ever will be able to fight with the All-powerful God and won victory over him. He is at all-time almighty.

But, to reward Jacob for his sublime faith in his omnipotence, and to make him understand that he had enough strength to confronting Esau, thirsty for revenge about his birthright which he had wrongly appropriated by cunning, he allowed him to achieve victory over him in this fierce fight to obtain his divine blessing. So it would be better for Esau to reconcile in advance with his brother Jacob. Fortunately, that's what he did. The God of mercy changed the furnace of hatred that was boiling in Esau's heart into a heart of a sheep, a heart filled with love and compassion for his brother.

The Lord has already punished Jacob for his sins, and received, with an open heart, his sincere repentance. Thus, he did not want Esau to inflict another punishment on him. For the Lord, punishment is not the product of hatred, of revenge, but of pure love, of a father's love for his son whom he wants to chastise for his own good. Proverbs 3:12 made it even clearer: **"The Lord disciplines the child he loves."**

CHAPTER FOUR
THe LORD Revealed HimSelf To MoSes

The necessity fell upon me to climb a few rungs in the life of Moses, before presenting the marvelous revelations of Almighty God to his servant. The word Moses translates to Moshe, 'From' or simply 'Out of the waters'. (Exodus 2:20). This word also has an Egyptian etymology, 'MS' meaning 'Child'; 'Son'. This is why, the daughter of Pharaoh named 'Son' the one whom she had drawn from the waters. But, I say: Moses was taken from death, first, and then from the waters since King Pharaoh was going to kill him before this marvelous event.

Biblical history has taught us that after about three hundred years, from the death of Joseph (1700-1400 BC), the seventy Hebrews who had settled in Gosen, were multiplied and became 600,000 men, not counting the women and children, otherwise this number could be multiplied and estimated at around three million people. They increased and became more and more numerous and powerful.

It is marvelous to see how the Lord multiplied and trained his people in the center of their bondage in Egypt, and how he sent them, in the midst of great danger and cruel suffering, a mighty deliverer, named: 'Moses'. At the time Joseph arrived in Egypt, the dynasty of kings who occupied Pharaoh's throne was called the 'Hyksos'. Pharaoh was a title given to all the kings of Egypt at that time; whether nationals or invaders.

This title went from 3150 to 1085 BC, a period of more than two thousand years. Thus, the Hyksos who were invaders from Asia between 1800-1600 BC was also called: The Pharaohs and they ruled for a period of two hundred years. Miraculously, this dynasty of Pharaoh was from the family of Abraham, and they were like the Hebrews, shepherds. It was under their reign that Joseph was acceded to the title of governor or viceroy where the Hebrews received all their protection. It was purely and simply divine providence.

Thanks to this dynasty of kings, the Hebrews multiplied and became very powerful. The native Egyptians united, fortified themselves, rose and expelled the Hyksos, that foreign dynasty, protector of the Hebrews. A new dynasty claimed the throne. This dynasty did not know Joseph and was unaware of the great deliverance that God granted to Egypt, through him. Who does not remember the very disturbing dream of King Pharaoh, when he saw, in a vision, the seven cows that were beautiful to look at and fat in flesh, and the seven cows that were ugly to look at and thin in flesh? The latter devoured the fat ones.

It seemed that the force of the dream woke him with a start. He fell asleep again and saw seven fat and beautiful ears, and seven thin and burnt ears. The latter engulfed the fat and beautiful ears. When he awoke, he was very troubled and hastily summoned to him all the magicians and all the wise men of Egypt. He took his time explaining these dreams to them, waiting for his troubled heart to enjoy a little relief, with a clear explanation. They became like people whose intellectual and mystical faculties are degraded by age. No one could explain anything. (**Read Genesis 41:1-8**)

Now, he has been told of a young Hebrew, a slave of the chief of the guards, who gives an easy explanation to dreams, however difficult they may be. Pharaoh summoned him. He explained his situation to him. Before giving an explanation to his dreams, Joseph let him know that it will not come from him, but from the Lord, the Omniscient. After hearing the same scenario that he presented to the magicians and sages, Joseph said to him: "The two dreams are analogous. They mean the same thing.

God warns you what he is going to do. He is going to bring seven years of plenty and seven years of drought. The years of famine will be so intense that the years of plenty will be forgotten. And, since the dream was repeated a second time, God will not take time to execute it". Joseph gave him this advice: to prevent a national desolation, the king will have all the products of these good years collected: heaps of wheat, supplies in towns. These provisions will be in reserve during the seven years of famine. This will save the country from certain destruction. The king obeyed and the country was spared. (Genesis 41:14-36)

How did this new dynasty ignore such deliverance that God granted to Egypt, through Joseph? Either way, the new kingdom ignored it, and took a dim view of the dizzying growth and multiplication of the population of the Israelites. The king feared that this unbridled growth would form a nation in itself and would join one or more allied nations of the kingdom to revolt and come out of Egypt. To prevent the fulfillment of this event which would prove very disastrous against his kingdom, the new king took the following steps:

He appeared before his people and expressed his concerns: "Here are the children of Israel who form a people more numerous and more powerful than us".

We have a solution to this problem that threatens our security: "Let us go! Let us show ourselves skilful with regard to it! Let us prevent this increase, and that, if there is a war, they do not join our enemies, to fight us and then leave the country!"

"Let us appoint taskmasters over them, so that he may build the cities of Pithom and Ramses, to serve as warehouses for Pharaoh". And, since the more they were overwhelmed, the more they multiplied, the Egyptians expelled and subjected them to a form of servitude even more degrading than that of animals. They were drained physically and mentally through laborious tasks involving clay and brick-making, as well as various other demanding duties and by all the works of the field, added to cruel punishments even for the most trivial infractions. Pharaoh was not yet satisfied.

Thus, he called to him, Schiphra and Pua, the midwives of the Hebrews, to order them:

"When you give birth to the women of the Hebrews, and you see them on the seats, if it is a boy, let him die; if it's a girl, let her live".

But the midwives feared God, and did not do what the king had told them, and they let the children live. The king called them and said, "Why did you do this; why did you let the children live?" They answered, "It is because the women of the Hebrews are not like the Egyptians; they are strong and give birth before the midwife arrives".

God does well to the midwives and the people multiplied and became very numerous. Because the midwives had had fear of God, God made their houses prosper. Then Pharaoh gave this order to all his people:

"You shall throw into the river every boy that is born, and you shall let all girls". (**Read Exodus 1:6-22**)

It was then that the mother of Moses, being in Egypt and unable to bear the thought of losing such a beautiful, admirable child, hid him for three months.

Obsessed with the feeling that he was going to be discovered soon, she decided not to hide him anymore. She placed him in a box of rushes and deposited it among the reeds, on the edge of the river (The Nile). His sister stood at a distance to watch him and see what would happen to him. The providence of God sent Pharaoh's daughter to swim on the side of the river where the child was. She saw the crate among the reeds, and she sent her servant take it off and bring it to him. She opened it and saw the child crying. She had pity on him, and said: **"He is a child of the Hebrews!"**

So the child's sister said to Pharaoh's daughter, "Do you want me to fetch you a nurse from among the Hebrew women to nurse the child?" "Certainly," she replied! And the girl went to get the child's mother. Pharaoh's daughter said to her, "Take this child away and suckle it for me; I will give you your salary". The woman took the child and nursed him. When he grew up, his mother brought him to Pharaoh's daughter, and he treated him like a son. She gave him the name of Moses, because, she said, "I took him out of the waters."

But why did Almighty God allow such cruel servitude to a people He so loved? No one can question an eternally powerful God. Mysteriously, he sometimes chooses a small number to share a fraction of his secrets. This is what he revealed to me concerning the reasons for the servitude of his people:

a) To remind him that the land of Egypt is not the one he promised to Isaac.
b) To arouse in them a desire to return to the Promised Land.
c) To divert the plan of the Egyptians who killed the male children of the Hebrews with the intention of marrying the Israelite daughters and that they become one people: "The Egyptian people". Moses was told at some point in his life that he was descended from the Israelites.

Having grown up, he went to his brothers, and witnessed their hard work. He saw an Egyptian who struck a Hebrew from among his brothers. He looked left and right, and seeing that there was no one, he killed the Egyptian and hid him in the sand; he went out the next day; and behold two Hebrews were quarreling. He said to the one who was wrong: "Why do you strike your neighbor?" And this man replied, "Who made you ruler and judge over us? Are you thinking of killing me like you killed the Egyptian?" Having discovered that the thing is known, Moses was afraid that Pharaoh, once informed, would have sought to kill him. So, to save his life, he retired to Midian. That's where the Lord was going to reveal himself to him, and he will have chosen him to be the mighty deliverer of his people. Having arrived there, he observed the seven daughters of Reuel who had come to water their father's flock.

Shepherds arrived to water their flocks as well. They hunted these young girls, even before accomplishing their mission. Moses defended them and made their flock drink. When they got home, they told their father about the happy event that had just happened. He, therefore encouraged them to seek out the benefactor to thank him and offer him food. He decided to stay at the Reuel's house, who became his father-in-law by giving him the hand of his eldest daughter, Zipporah. (**Read Exodus 2:11-21**)

Meanwhile, the people of Israel were groaning in the most horrible bondage, and shouting loudly. The compassionate God heard their cries and remembered his covenant with Abraham, Isaac and Jacob. This is how God revealed himself to him, in the middle of a burning bush, and called him: "Moses, Moses!" And he answered;" The LORD-God said unto him, draw not nigh hither, put off thy shoes, for the place where you stand is holy ground". And, he added: "I am the God of your fathers, the God of Abraham, the God of Isaac and the God of Jacob". The Lord continued, "I have seen the suffering of my people who are in Egypt, and I have heard the cries their oppressors made them utter, for I understand their pain. I have come down to deliver them out of the hand of the Egyptians, and bring them out of this land into a good and wide land, into a land where milk and honey flow in the places inhabited by the Canaanites, the Hittites, the Amorites, the Parse, the Hivites and the Jebusites. Now go, I will send you to Pharaoh, and you will bring my people, the children of Israel, out of Egypt".

Moses, stricken with terror, did not hide his fears, and openly declared to the Lord the trouble of his heart: "Who am I to go to Pharaoh and bring the children of Israel out of Egypt?" God says, "I will be with you; and this will be for you the sign that it is I who sent you" (**Read Exodus 2:23-25 and 3:1-12**).

CHAPTER FIVE

THE FURIOUS ANTAGONISM BETWEEN SATAN, THE GREAT TEMPTER, & JESUS, THE FOUNDER OF THE NEW DOCTRINE

Surely the great tempter of humanity, Satan the Devil, knew that the existence of the church in his earthly kingdom would injure his power among the sons of men. This is why he ruthlessly attacked its founder or its divine-human Architect Jesus of Nazareth, who is at the same time the Great Architect of the universe. Because of this, he sought to kill him as soon as he was born, by the bloody hand of King Herod. First, after having inquired about the open declaration of the Magi from the East: "Where is the king of the Jews who has just been **born?**"(Matthew 2:3)

The Bible tells us that Herod was troubled and all Jerusalem with him. And I deduce from this: Herod was disturbed at the thought that the Child Jesus, born king, was about to usurp his power; and Jerusalem was troubled because of the confusion between the two kings: King Jesus and King Herod.

Then, as a puppet of Satan, King Herod could invent all kinds of tricks to eliminate the divine Master or the Child Jesus. They knew very well that the chief priests and scribes were well versed in the knowledge of laws and prophets. They were commonly called, doctors of the law. On the other hand, King Herod gathered them together and inquired from them, according to the prophecy, of the exact birthplace of the new King. They declared, in all truth: "At Bethlehem, in Judea."

This is what the prophet Micah prophesied in the book that bears his name:

"And you, Bethlehem, land of Judah, you are certainly not the least among the main cities of Judah, because out of you will come a leader who will feed Israel, my people?" (Micah 5:1)

In addition to this, Herod summoned, in secret, the Magi, astrologers from the East, to astutely inquire from them, how long the star had been shining. Then he sent them to Bethlehem, saying,

"Come on, and get some exact information about the little child. When you find him, let me know, so that I too may go and worship him". (Matthew 2:7-8)

After having listened to the disloyal requests of the king, they continued their mission, that of seeing the Child and adoring him. In reality, the star led them to the manger, the exact place where the Child Jesus was, and it stopped. They felt great joy. They entered it. They saw the little Child and his mother. With a heart filled with joy and gratitude, they offered him, as gifts, gold, frankincense and myrrh.

In their innocence, they were about to go back to Jerusalem, to answer the king's demands. It was then that they were divinely warned, by a holy angel, not to return to Herod, who had no intention of worshiping the Child-King, but killing him.

The Magi obeyed, without compulsion, the angel of God, ignoring King Herod's malicious request and went another way. After realizing that the Magi were ignoring his request and discovered his treacherous intent, he roared in anger, and ordered all children two years and above to be killed, hoping that he will kill, at all costs, the child Jesus. The result was a national distress, a birth pang, and it was also the fulfillment of the prophecy announced by Isaiah, in Isaiah 40:3. The whole story can also be read in Matthew 2:1-18. The tearing of Rachel's womb was laid bare in **Matthew 2:18:**

"Cries were heard at Rama,
Tears and great lamentations:

Rachel mourns her children,
And did not want to be comforted,
Because they are no more".

Jesus was not among the slain children. So Herod could not kill King Jesus, and Satan failed in his first attempt. For, Jesus was covered by the power of his Father's right hand. I want to report to everyone that Satan always proves to be a stubborn, wicked, persistent and ruthless attacker, but not the big winner. Indeed, he pursued my Master to Calvary, but without laurels.

In reality, Jesus was crucified. He was dead and he was buried. Satan claimed victory, because he hurt Jesus' heel. But, what a folly and what an audacity! Whether he was a renowned warrior or Lucifer, Satan knew very well that he could not kill the 'God with us'. No one has power over him except his Father, since he has the power to lay down his life and to take it up again. Therefore, he declared these irrefutable words in **John 10:17-18:**

"The Father loves me, because I give my life, in order to take it back. No one takes it from me, but I give it of myself; I have the power to give it, and I have the power to take it back: such is the order I received from my Father"

Indeed, between the years 790 and 700 of the prophetic era, the prophet Isaiah announced, by the Spirit, in **Isaiah 53:5:**

"But he was wounded for our transgressions, crushed for our iniquities; The chastisement that gives us peace fell on him, And it is by his stripes that we are healed".

Our sins and iniquities condemned us before the justice of God, and when our death sentence was pronounced, Jesus decided to die in our place, so that we might have life. What a love! He deserves our eternal gratitude.

Furthermore, who could have fought him? Indeed, heaven is his throne and the earth his footstool. This is why the earth trembled in its foundations, when the executioners placed him in its bosom. From the first second, the earth began to shake. But alas, it had to endure this intense heat, this devouring fire which consumed it, since the divine Master himself had prophesied that he was to remain there for three days. (**Matthew 24:1-8**)

Thus, three days later that is, a Sunday morning in the year thirty-third of the christian era, Mary Magdalene; Mary the mother of James and Salomé bought aromatics, a kind of special and expensive perfume, to embalm the tomb of Jesus.

They were deeply grateful for all that he had done for humanity, but also and above all for the countless benefits that they themselves had received from him. With hearts gnawed with sadness, they went to the sepulcher. When they got there, they found two men in resplendent clothes sitting on his grave.

Seized with fear, they lowered their heads, but the angels of God said to them: "Why do you seek among the dead the living one. This Jesus you are looking for is not here, He is risen". And the holy angels recalled them, "remember how he speak unto you, when he was yet in Galilee, and said, The Son of man must be delivered into the hands of sinners, he will be crucified and that he will rise again on the third day ", and they remembered it. (**Matthew 24:1-8**)

One of the beneficiaries of the resurrection, certainly the apostle Paul, was to say one day:

"Death has been swallowed up in victory.
O death, where is your victory?
O death, where is your sting?"
(**1 Corinthians 15:54b-55**)

After these laurels and these prowess, that is to say victory over the relentless attacks of Satan; victory over sin; victory over death, Jesus Christ finally founded his church, at Pentecost, in the person of the Holy Spirit.

Now, Satan, in his desperation, his outrageous audacity or his bewilderment, has launched a mortal and definitive blow against this church which he thought to be at the same time very young, very weak and very vulnerable. He has sworn to pursue it until the return of Jesus Christ, by repeated assaults, and the most terrifying. Could it be, within his bounds, that he could not have been informed of the prophetic words of the Son of God, written in the book of life? *"The gates of Hades will not prevail against it"*. (Matthew 16:18b)

Henceforth, he unleashed a merciless persecution against this young but powerful church, immured by the power of the right hand of the great Architect of its construction. It is the reed that will be bent by the flaming arrows of the tempter, but never broken.

The persecution was so intense that the disciples saw the sword of Damocles hovering over their heads. They were therefore unable to stay in Jerusalem. For this, the Bible informs us, that all the disciples were scattered, to take refuge in the countries of Judea and Samaria; not, to abandon the gospel, but to preach it with still more conviction, authority and boldness. But, the apostles braved these atrocious persecutions, and remained in Jerusalem, at the cost of their lives.

A brother approached me one day and asked me this impertinent question: "Pastor, how is it that all the other disciples scattered to save themselves from this cruel persecution, while the apostles had such courage to remain among those wicked persecutors in Jerusalem in the face of such an imminent danger?" To which I replied: first, Jesus promised them to receive direct power from the Holy Spirit: "The Holy Spirit coming upon you, and you shall be my witnesses in Jerusalem, in all Judea, in Samaria, and unto to the ends of the earth" **(Acts 1:8)** Second, they received a formal command from the founder of the new doctrine or simply, the founder of the church: "Go not to the heathen, and enter not into the cities of the Samaritans, but go rather to the lost sheep of the house of Israel".

CHAPTER SIX

The Lord Revealed Himself To Philip

During this forced dispersion of the disciples, Phillip, the deacon-evangelist, and one of the fugitives from the painful persecution of the church of Jesus-Christ, went to Samaria and preached Christ there. Filled with the Holy Spirit, he performed many miracles there. It was there that Almighty God revealed Himself to him. For while he was working these miracles in the country of Samaria, an Ethiopian minister, a convinced believer in the new doctrine, minister of Candice, queen of Ethiopia, rushed to go to Jerusalem for the sole purpose of worshiping the one true God. On his way back, thirsty for the knowledge of the living God, he was reading Isaiah 53 or more precisely, **Isaiah 53:7-8** where it says:

"He was abused and oppressed
And he did not open his mouth,
Like a lamb led to the slaughter,
Like a sheep dumb before those who shear it;
He did not open his mouth.
He was taken away by anguish and chastisement;
And among those of his generation, who believed
That he was cut off from the land of the living
And smitten for the sins of my people?"

The Eunuch or the Ethiopian minister had difficulty in understanding the passage he was reading. The omniscient, omnipresent and omnipotent God, who searches the hearts and the loins, soon, detected the ardent thirst which withered the minister's heart to belong to him, revealed himself to Philip by detaching a heavenly delegate, his holy angel, to order him: "Rise up and go southward on the way from Jerusalem to Gaza" Acts 8:26, the exact place where the Ethiopian minister, the christian aspirant was reading with difficulty of understanding the passage from **Isaiah 53:**

Then, with a face lit up with joy, and a heart freed from all prejudice, Philip opened his mouth and easily began, through the passage in question, to explain to him that it was about Jesus who agreed to abandon his kingdom, his riches and eternal glory, inherited from his Father; that he accepted to descend on this earth of sin to accept to let fall on him, our transgressions, our iniquities, so that whoever believes that he is the Son of God and is baptized has eternal life.

As they continued, they encountered water, and the minister exclaimed, "Here is water, what prevents me from being baptized?"

And Philip answers: If you believe with all your heart, it is possible. And the eunuch continued: **"I believe that Jesus is the Son of God".**

Overjoyed, Philip and the Eunuch descended into the water, and Philip baptized him. In a word, Philip explained to the Ethiopian minister, the difficult passage to understand; the minister believed and soon became an official member of the Christian family.

This miracle had occurred after the revelation of God to Philip, in collaboration with the obedience and humility of the Ethiopian minister who sincerely reserved a place for Jesus in his heart.

CHAPTER SEVEN

THE LORD REVEALED HIMSELF TO SAUL OF TARSUS & ANANIAS

S aul of Tarsus, who later became the Apostle Paul, was one of the most ruthless persecutors of the Church of Jesus Christ. He and his wicked group made a firm decision to forcibly destroy this new doctrine or gospel of Jesus Christ, which was about to confuse the people, and even the whole world, for the simple fact that this new doctrine required everyone to leave the things of this age of darkness, which would lead to death, to hell, to turn to the things above, to Jesus Christ, which would lead to eternal life.

Jesus-Christ, who is the author of the new doctrine, initiated this formal and imperative command in Matthew 28:19-20: "Go, make disciples of all nations, baptizing them in the name of the Father, and of the Son, and of the Holy Spirit, and teach them to observe all that I have commanded you. And behold, I am with you always, until the end of the world".

Saul of Tarsus was born in Tarsus, a city in Cilicia, occupied by Rome. So he was a Roman citizen by birth. He was, however, of Jewish descent, brought up by one of the most eminent of the Jewish rabbis of the time, Gamaliel, doctor of the law. Indeed, Paul said, himself, in **Acts 22:3**:

"I am a Jew, born in Tarsus in Cilicia; but I was brought up in this city, and instructed at the feet of Gamaliel in the exact knowledge of the law of our fathers, being full of zeal for God, as you all are today".

He then added in **Philippians 3:5-6:**

"I, circumcised on the eighth day, of the race of Israel, of the tribe of Benjamin, a Hebrew born of Hebrews; as to the law, a Pharisee; as to zeal, persecutor of the Church; blameless in the justice of the law".

As a young man, Saul was admitted among the great. His superior intelligence earned him the title of member of the Sanhedrin at youthful age, the most respected Jewish governing body of his time, while Ananias was a simple christian, without any fame, almost totally unknown to the great society. He wouldn't even have dared or had the opportunity to meet the apostle Paul for a lifetime, let alone to untie the straps of his shoes. Yet, O divine mystery! It was he whom the Lord was going to choose to lay his hand on the head of this powerful, tall and formidable man.

The priests, the magistrates and Saul of Tarsus himself had hoped that, through their vigilant efforts and cruel persecutions, they would succeed in eradicating forever this new doctrine or this terror-spreading Christianity which they compared to heresy, a pernicious sect, because they were blind leading the blind or blinded by the great darkness of Satan.

To make sure of the success of their special and imperative mission, this group chose the young, the furious, the inflexible Saul of Tarsus, to be in charge. By bitter zeal, he has already led quite a few christians, men and women to the tribunals which would have condemned them to imprisonment, torture and death.

So then, after being informed that the Christians of Damascus were lining up more and more around the new doctrine, Saul of Tarsus, still breathing threats and murder against the disciples of the Lord, hastened to go to the high priest and asked him for letters of recommendation for the synagogues of Damascus, so that, if he found partisans of the new doctrine, men or women, he could arrest them and brought them back bound to Jerusalem.

After having received the authorization from the chief priests, Saul of Tarsus, thinking he was endowed with invincible power, threw himself like a hare into this reckless journey, completely forgetting the salutary advice of Gamaliel, in **Acts 5:38:**

"And now I say to you: Do not concern yourself with these men any longer, and let them go. If this enterprise comes from men, it will destroy itself; but if it comes from God, you cannot destroy it. Do not run the risk of having fought against God".

Gamaliel was inspired from above, in formulating these words. For on the way, and not far from Damascus, towards the middle of the day, the Apostle Paul himself later reported, suddenly a dazzling light shone around him and his companions. He fell to the ground and he heard a voice saying to him:

"Saul, Saul, why are you persecuting me?" He hastened to answer: "who are you, Lord?" And the answer was: "I am Jesus whom you persecute". In other words, christians are the apples of my eyes. Don't touch them! For whoever seeks to fight them, will fight me first. And who can kick at my goads? Who can resist my almighty strength?

Smitten by the lion of the tribe of Judah, Jesus of Nazareth, The general of generals and the warrior of the centuries, Saul of Tarsus had immediately become a blind handicap who had to be taken to Damascus. The Lord spoke to Ananias, his humble servant or disciple, to go into the street called the Straight, and seeks in the house of Judas a certain one named Saul of Tarsus.

For he prayed and he saw in a vision a man named Ananias who came in and laid his hands on him to recover his sight. After legitimate disputes with the Lord, on the ground that Saul has done so much wrong to his people, Ananias finally obeyed his divine Master, and he left. Arriving at the house of Saul of Tarsus, he imposed his hand on his head, and, at the same time, he recovered his sight.

In truth, the Lord our God, is the only true God, the only God who exists on earth as it is in heavens. When he decides to save and deliver those he loves, he has to open his mouth, and everything becomes calm around him: The wind, the storm and the fury of Saul of Tarsus.

CHAPTER EIGHT

The Lord Revealed Himself To Cornellius & Peter

C ornelius was a centurion, (leader of a hundred soldiers) in the Roman army. He was very rich and belonged to a high social class. A pagan by birth, he was blessed to know the one true God through personal information. For, before Jesus Christ, the Jews had no relationship with the pagans. Devoting himself, certainly, to the disinterested search for the one true God, Cornelius turned himself to the study of the laws and the prophets and became a proselyte. After gaining a convincing knowledge of the one true God, he worshiped Him with all his heart. He proved that the love and fear of God pressed his heart, by his interest in the poor and in prayer. He was very famous for his generosity and his exemplary life among the pagans. His reputation reached to the ears of the Jews.

For, the word of God bore excellent testimony of him. In **Acts 10:1-2** we read:

"There was in Caesarea a man named Cornelius, a centurion in the so-called Italian cohort. This man was pious and God-fearing, with his entire household; he gave many alms to the people, and prayed to God continually".

Being a pagan, Cornelius expected no blessing from God, according to the Jews. Thus, for them, the God of Abraham, Isaac and Jacob belongs only to the Jewish people. Indeed, Corneilius had three spiritual qualities, of which the Almighty God could not ignore: the fear of God, the love of justice and the love of neighbor. With these spiritual qualities, the Lord accepted Cornelius as a worker in his harvest; he presented him, at the same time, the greatest honor, by sending his holy angel to bring him a direct message which made the eternal joy of his heart. Upon meeting him, the angel gave him the message recorded in **Acts 10:4b-6:**

"Your prayers and your alms have gone up before God, and he has remembered them. Now send men to Joppa, and ask Simon, surnamed Peter to come; he is lodged with a certain Simon, currier, whose house is near the sea".

Convinced that the presence of Peter would abound his house with inexhaustible graces, Cornelius, in his altruistic spirit, invited his relatives and close friends, on this happy occasion, to come and share with him these abundant blessings. And I deduce: Cornelius was not only a man of faith and generosity, but a man deprived of any spirit of selfishness. He obeys the angel without constraint. When the latter was gone, the centurion called two of his most faithful servants and a pious soldier from among those who were attached to his person, and after having told them everything, he sent them to Joppa.

O power! O divine mystery! After taking leave of Cornelius, the angel went directly to Peter at Joppa. The latter was praying at that time on the roof of his house, and the scripture tells us that he was hungry and wanted to eat. While the food was being prepared, he fell into ecstasy. In his vision the apostle saw heaven opened up and an object like a large tablecloth tied by the four corners, which descended towards the earth where were all the quadrupeds and the birds of the sky . And this voice was heard: "Get up Peter, kill and eat". But, Peter replied, "No, Lord! For I have never eaten anything filthy and unclean". And for the second time the voice came to him: "What God declares pure, do not regard it as defiled." This happens until the third time, and immediately he was taken up into heaven.

While Peter was meditating on the meaning of the vision, the men sent by Cornelius arrived at Joppa, sought his house, and presented themselves at the door. They asked eagerly and aloud if that was where Simon, nicknamed Peter, was staying.

O infinite wisdom! The Lord who knows all the movements of the heart of man, knew well that Peter was not going to receive the men who had come from Caesarea, whom they considered to be Isolated and impure. This is why he sent his angel in advance to warn him: "Behold, three men are seeking to meet with you; get up, get down and go with them without hesitation". Fact is I sent them.

Struggling against the rising tide of his prejudices Peter was obliged to obey the order of the divine Master. He got down and went to those men sent by Cornelius and said to them, "Behold, I am the one you are looking for. What is the motive that brings you here?" They, therefore told him of their divine mission and spoke with pride of the remarkable qualities of their amiable leader "Cornelius". They said to Peter, "Cornelius, a centurion, a just man and fearing God", and of whom Jewish nation bears good witness, has been divinely warned by a holy angel, to bring you into his house to hear your words"

Struck with awe and reverence towards God, the apostle obeyed without hesitation, and promised to go with these men. He brought them in and lodged them. The next day he got up very early and went with them, also taking with him some brothers from Joppa; without a doubt, brothers who loved the Lord and attached themselves to his ministry. When Peter arrived at Caesarea, at the house of Cornelius, this rich and powerful man humbled himself, to such an extent that he put himself kneeling to receive the apostle, a sign of respect for a leader whom God has anointed, and Peter had not accepted this kind of reception, but appreciated it with great humility. He lifted him up, with these words that made my whole being shudder, made me even more humble and increased my love for my God and his people: "Get up", said Peter to Cornelius, "For I too am a man like you", a sign of sincere humility and spiritual cleansing. Continuing his conversation with Cornelius, who was then his bitter enemy and rejection of Jewish society, for his pagan identity; today, intimate friend and brother, by the justice of God, the power of the gospel and his Christian identity.

Peter entered his home and found many people gathered together, thirsty to hear him. He sincerely reminded them: "You know that it is forbidden for a Jew to bind himself with a foreigner or a heathen and to enter his house; but, God taught me not to regard any man as defiled and impure". It was then that Peter asked Cornelius why he had sent for him. And Cornelius replied, with this attitude of humility that followed him:

"Four days ago, at this hour, I was praying in my house at the ninth hour; and behold, a man arrayed in a bright robe came before me, and said, Cornelius, your prayer has been heard, and God has remembered your alms. Send therefore to Joppa, and bring Simon, surnamed Peter; he is lodged in Simon's house, currier, by the sea. Immediately I sent to you, and you did well to come. Now, therefore, we are all before God, to hear all that the Lord has commanded you to tell us".

Peter, marveling at the omniscience of God, and his immeasurable love for the men he created in his image and his likeness and also, who recognized him as their only true God, cried out:
"Truly I know that God has no respect for anyone, but in every nation he who fears him and does justice is pleasing to him". (Acts 10: 34-35)

Then, in the presence of this audience eager to hear him or of this august assembly, Peter presented Jesus Christ, as savior of the world, his exemplary and perfect life. While he was subject to all kinds of temptations, sufferings for you and me, but he has never sinned. He told him of the miracles he had performed; of the cures he wrought; of the betrayal of which he was the victim. He also spoke with emotion that he was arrested, crucified and put to death. But why, Jesus who was the Son of God and God himself, accepted all the insults from the hands of the ungodly? He accepted all of this out of his great love for us, his beloved creatures. He accepted everything just to pay the price for our sins, our iniquities, not only to deliver us from death, but also and above all to give us eternal life; that he was raised and ascended into heaven, to be our advocate before the Father.

As Peter exalted Jesus as the world's only savior and only hope, spiritual fire burned in his heart. Suddenly the talk was interrupted by the outpouring of the Holy Spirit. As Peter spoke these words, the Holy Spirit descended on all who listened to him. All the faithful circumcised who were with Peter were amazed that the gift of the Holy Spirit was also poured out on the heathen or the uncircumcised. They heard them speaking in tongues and glorified God. This is why the apostle Paul said in **1 Corinthians 7:19:**

"Circumcision is nothing, and uncircumcision is nothing, but keeping the commandments of God is everything".

Then Peter exclaimed, in Acts 10:47: "Can we refuse the water of baptism to those who have received the Holy Spirit as well as we?" And he commanded that they be baptized in the name of the Lord Jesus. Alleluia! Cornelius and his house, who had hitherto been considered pagans, impur, barbarians, and uncircumcised, had henceforth become, fellow citizens of the saints, new members of the house of God. Who would resist this new doctrine? Who would argue against this mighty Christianity?

Powerful enough, to cast out seven demons from Mary of Magdala's head (Mark 16:9).

Powerful enough, to heal the daughter of Jarius and the woman who had been sick for twelve years (Matthew 9:18-26).

Powerful enough, to resuscitate Lazarus (John 11:1-46).

Powerful enough, to open the eyes of Bartimaeus, the blind beggar (Mark 10:46-5).

Powerful enough, to heal a sick person for thirty-eight years, at the house of mercy, the pool of Bethesda (John 5:1-1)

Powerful enough, to convince Peter to meet Cornelius the uncircumcised, the rejection of the Jewish nation, an irreconcilable enemy.

Powerful enough, finally to forgive our sins, our iniquities, and heal our infirmities and give us eternal life.

All this evidence of God's revelation to fallen man whom he created in his own image and likeness was to convince those who are weak in the faith and, dear readers, was it not a strange thing that the Lord had revealed himself to me, Morales, the last of his disciples, as chosen servant, to write what he has done for me and what he has revealed to me, building up those whom he has called into his kingdom.

CHAPTER NINE
The Origin & The Growth Of My Life In Christ

My father had informed me that at the end of October 1958, a group of Christians arrived at our house whose compassionate mission was to pray for my mother, who was then seriously ill. It encouraged us to focus our faith on Christ. For, he says, it can lead to miracles and great blessings. We believed, and after a while we experienced the first miracle of my mother's healing. "You were five years old, my father reminded me, and that was when the entire household accepted Christ".

My father had two girls and a boy and my mother, three girls and a boy. My father's children were called: Adélucia, Edna and I, Morales, your servant; my mother's children were: Théana, Antoinette, Edna and Moralès. This genealogy has quite a small complication, but I will make it very clear to you, dear readers. My older sister Adélucia is not my mother's daughter. She was still a tender child when her mother died. She didn't even know her. During the first years of her life, she was cared for by my father. Later, she was raised by my father and my mother. Everyone loved her because she was exceptionally driven. She lived with my parents until her happy marriage. My mother's other two daughters do not belong to my father. Frankly speaking, I had no information. Indeed, at the time, parents did not speak to children of their past life. But, I could guess that she was divorced, abandoned or abused by the other spouse or partner. I was not interested in inquiring further information or exact information. That's not the purpose of the book.

Indeed, I could not receive additional information, since my father, my mother, my two half-sisters on my mother's side have already passed away. I am my parents only boy.

My father was gentle and humble of heart. He loved and respected everyone. He was honored by all people he knows. He was a counselor to many. His name was Fadéus Saintilus, nicknamed 'Fadé' by his parents and the elders; Magot by his brothers, sisters, children and close friends in his neighborhood. The younger generation called him 'Ton Magot' or 'Uncle Magot'. None of his children called him dad. All of us have followed our predecessors by also calling him 'Magot'. My father's friends used to call me 'Ti Fadé', which means 'Like father, like son'.

They deduced that I inherited all these qualities from my father: love of neighbor, humility, great character, spirit of service, compassion and so on. They also used to exclaim, approaching me: "My God, all your ways are like your father's", and I was proud of it.

To prove that what people said about me and my father is true, my father told me that I started to share everything I have with everybody and anybody at the age of two and that continues all my life.

Furthermore, in the 60's, about 15% of children went to school. Most of them started at the age of seven to seventeen years old. I feel that God took charge of me since I was in my mother's womb. He chose since then, because he knows, I will chose him for my God and serve him the rest of my life.

As I just said above, most of the kids in the 60's in my neighbourhood went to school at a late age. I could definitely be one of them. But, at the age of five, God's providence sent to us, kids, a mentor as an instructor who did a wonderful job in our life, and I will never forget him. When he discovered my gift, he encouraged my parents to send me in a regular school as soon as possible. They did, and I became a brilliant student for the rest of my school years.

The evidence of my calling started when I was eight years old. At this time, everyone in the neighbourhood was a child's protector. That's the blessing I received to go, at this very young age, everywhere in the neighbourhood, teaching the other kids. When the parents paid me 50 cents, it was a world of wealth for me. In fact, I shared it with the other kids. This mission owes me the title of 'professor Mora' since I was eight years old.

Indeed, I deeply loved my mother, but I was cemented to my father. I was for my father as Isaac was for Abraham and Joseph for Jacob. Although he loved all of his children, his preference for me was very obvious. He couldn't live without me and me, without him. He had a reclining chair, six feet high. When he came back from work, he would take a shower. After that, he ate something and climbed into his high chair for a good rest. I remember being four years old, and my father confirmed it to me, when I climbed on the bars of his chair to throw myself tenderly and confidently on his chest where, after five minutes, I was sleeping soundly. He later informed me that he used to take me with him in his chair from the age of three.

I continued to climb on it and sleep on his chest until I was six years old. It was then that he decided to buy a small chair for me and placed it next to his where I also felt comfortable and happy.

He had a special affection for Adélucia, my older sister and my second older sister, Edna. I used to say to my father : you love Adelucia more than us. He replied as a smart father: "I have three children, and I love you all equally. Same goes to your two other sister". He paid more attention to my older sister, for the following reasons: first, she was the eldest of his children; second, her mother had died, when she was only a year old and finally, she grew up alone with my father until the age of seven, when he met my mother and formed a new family.

In truth, we grew up in a very pleasant atmosphere where there was perfect peace, disturbed only by circumstances beyond our control. We lived in the fourth section of Limbé, in the north of Haiti, called Modieu. It was a picturesque and verdant little district, where the croaking of the rooster, the howling of the oxen, the meow of the cats, the neighing of the horse, the song of the nightingale, the blooming of the flowers of the fields, would have pushed the fervent Christians to exclaim with the Evangelist Luke, in **Luke 2:14:**

"Glory to God in the highest,
And peace on earth among men whom he accepts!"

It really was a beautiful neighborhood. It looked like it was there, the site of the Garden of Eden. Streams of water abounded there. There, there were trees and plants of all kinds, providing each faithfully, his food to their cultivators or owners. Among this multitude, we could distinguish:

Almond tree. Fruit tree (rosaceous), growing up 6 to 8 m high, with white flowers appearing early in spring and producing almonds. The pineapple. Semi-perennial low plant, cultivated in tropical regions which provide a fruit with a tasty pulp. Its large oblong fruit, surmounted by a bouquet, also bears its name.

Apple tree. Widespread tree (rosacea), cultivated for its fruit, the apple, or as an ornamental tree.

Apricot tree. Fruit tree (rosaceous) of the genus prunes, and whose fruit is the apricot, large fleshy fruit, sweet and tasty, whose smooth core contains an edible almond and whose pulp is used in jams and pastries.

Asparagus. Perennial cultivated plant (lily), of the genus asparagus, whose young shoots are eaten, cooked.

Avocado tree. Fruit tree (Lauraceous) of hot regions, whose fruit is the avocado.

Bamboo. Cultivated plant whose leaves, roots, tubers, fruits, seeds are consumed, depending on the species; consumed part of this plant.

Banana tree. Very large perennial herb (musaceous) of the equatorial regions, with huge leaves, and whose fruit is the banana.

Bean. Annual or perennial (Papilionaceae), climbing plant, with trifoliate leaves, many varieties of which are grown for its pods (green bean) or for its seeds, which are very common vegetables.

Beet. Biennial plant of the Chenopodiaceous family, which gives the first year a fleshy root and goes to seed the second year.

Cabbage. Name given to various species of plants, of the cruciferous family, forming a large number of varieties cultivated for human and animal consumption.

Carrot. Plant cultivated for its edible root of cylindrical shape, more or less elongated, of red color.

Cassava. Tropical food plant (euphorbiaceous) with edible roots, from which tapioca is obtained.

Celery. Cultivated, edible biennial plant. A distinction is made between celery root, the fleshy root of which is eaten, and celeriac, the voluminous root of which is eaten.

Chamomile. Fragrant plant of which several species are consumed in infusion for their digestive virtues.

Cherry tree. Fruit tree (rosacea), with white flowers, of the prunus genus, whose fruit is the cherry.

Citrus. Small tree in warm temperate regions, whose fruit has the structure of an orange. (Citrus fruits are classified in the genus citrus).

Cocoa tree. Small tree (sterculiaceae) from the undergrowth of tropical regions, native to South America, cultivated mainly in Africa, for the production of cocoa.

Coconut tree. Palm of tropical shores, with a relatively frail trunk, up to 25 m high, whose edible fruit is the coconut.

Coffee tree. Shrub (Rubiaceae) grown in tropical regions for its fruit, coffee.

Corn. Large cereal (grass) of American origin, with a strong stem bearing a female ear formed of grains placed in very tight rows.

Cotton. Plant (malvaceae) tropical herbaceous or ligneous, cultivated for its oilseeds and its fruit, covered with cellulosic hairs, or cotton.

Cress. Cruciferous grass of humid places, with leaves with round and unequal leaflets, edible raw or cooked, rich in vitamin C, with small white flowers with round petals, which are grown in watercress beds.

Cucumber. Annual cucurbit, with yellow flowers and long creeping stems, cultivated for its fruit. Fruit of this plant, oblong, containing many seeds, appreciated for its crunchy, watery and refreshing flesh.

Garlic. Plant (lily) whose bulbs (heads of garlic) are formed of cloves (cloves of garlic) which have a strong smell and a pungent taste, which makes them sought after for seasoning. (Gifted with an antibiotic power due to garlicine and alisine, garlic, also has a hypotensive action.)

Hyacinth. Bulbous liliaceous with very decorative, fragrant, spring-like cluster flowers, many varieties of which are grown in gardens or in apartments, sometimes without soil.

Jasmine. Shrub (oleaceous) erect or sarmentose with very fragrant white, yellow or reddish flowers, with a tubular corolla, united in cymes or in clusters. Perfume that we get from these flowers.

Leek. Cultivated plant (lily), eaten as a vegetable, consisting of sheathing leaves, forming at their base a cylinder of which the buried part, white and tender, is the most appreciated.

Lemon tree. Tree of the citrus group which produces lemons, especially grown in regions with a subtropical Mediterranean climate.

Lettuce. Cultivated (compound) annual plant with rapid growth, the most common of the plants used in salads.

Mango. Fruit tree (anacardiaceous) from tropical regions with well-marked seasons. (These are American hybrids that supply the commercial mango) It produces the mango, a fleshy, edible fruit with an adherent stone.

Melon. Creeping annual plant (cucurbitaceous) cultivated for its fruits, requiring a lot of heat and light, of which there are many varieties. Fruit of this plant, round or oval, with green to yellow or light brown skin and sweet and fragrant, orange to greenish flesh.

Mint. Very fragrant (lipped) plant, usually hairy, very common in damp places. Syrup, extract, flavor made from mint.

Orange tree. Tree of the citrus group, with evergreen leaves, of the genus citrus, cultivated in warm regions and which produces oranges. (The United States, Brazil, Spain, Italy are the main producing countries.)

Palm. Monocotyledonous tree with a trunk (stripe) little or not branched, with upper foliage formed of compound leaves, which are pinnate or webbed depending on the species, whose bud or palm kernel cabbage is consumed as a vegetable. (The palm family, or Palmaceae, has more than 4,000 species.)

Parsley. Small annual or biennial umbelliferous, with finely ribbed stem, very cut leaves, which serves as a condiment and garnish.

Pea. Plant (Papilionaceous) cultivated for its seeds, intended for human or animal food, and as fodder. Seed of this plant.

Peach tree. Fruit tree (rosaceous) 3 to 5 m high, grown in temperate regions, and of which there are many varieties of the prunus genus and whose fruit is the peach.

Pear tree. Fruit tree (rosaceous) of temperate regions, producing the pear.

Pepper. Name given to several plants (solanaceous) whose fruit is used as a condiment or as a vegetable. Its fruit is sweet or pungent.

Plum tree. Fruit tree of the prunus genus cultivated for its fruit, the plum.

Potato. Plant (solanaceae) cultivated for its tubers, rich in starch, used for human and animal food and from which starch is obtained. Edible tuber of this plant.

Pumpkin. Common name for several species of cucurbits including the Touraine pumpkin, a large squash (head) producing fruits that can weigh 50 kg.

Radish. Plant of which there are various varieties (small radishes turnip radishes, black radishes) cultivated for their edible fleshy root. The root of this plant.

Rice. Usual name of a grass of the genus oryza, a cereal very widespread in hot regions and whose grains are widely used for human food. Seeds of this plant.

Shallot. Vegetable plant, close to the onion, whose bulb is used as a condiment.

Spinach. Name given to plants providing leaves that are eaten like spinach (orach, bonne-dame, amarante-ansérine, ansérine bon-henri, tetragone or New Zealand spinach, sorrel-patience, baselle).

Squash. Vegetable and ornamental plant (cucurbitaceous), with a long climbing stem and large orange flowers, of which there are many cultivated forms (zucchini, whose fruit is picked when young; pumpkin, with very large fruit with orange-yellow flesh used in soups; pumpkin; squash).

Strawberries tree. Creeping perennial plant cultivated and existing in the woods in the wild state, the edible fruit of which is the strawberry. (Strawberries are perennial plants usually bearing stolons, trifoliate leaves, white flowers, family Rosaceous.)

Sugar cane. Tropical plant 2 to 5 meters tall, cultivated for the sugar extracted from its stem.

Sunflower. Tall (composite) annual plant, with large yellow inflorescence which turns towards the sun, cultivated for its seeds which provide quality edible oil and a meal rich in protein, used for livestock feed.

Tomato. Annual herbaceous plant (solanaceae), whose cultivation is widespread and whose fleshy fruit is consumed in a wide variety of forms. The tomato (Lycopersicum esculentum), native to the Andes and Central America, has become one of the most important Verbena. Herb or sub-shrub with small lilac or blue flowers, calyx and tubular corolla. (Hybrid verbena is grown for herbal teas and as an ornamental. Verbena officinal is antispasmodic and tonic; lemon verbena is used in digestive fusions.)

Tulip. Bulbous liliaceous with large and beautiful solitary vase-shaped flowers, industrially cultivated. (The flower shows six large petoloid pieces or petals of very diverse color, depending on the crop variety.)

Vine. Climbing shrub (vitaceae), a cultivated species of which produces grapes.

Violet. Is said of a pigment, a dye or a lacquer whose color constitutes one of the visible limits of the spectrum of decomposition of sunlight and approaches that of the flower called: 'Violet'.

Walnut. Large tree (juglandaceae) in temperate regions, which is grown for its fruit, the nut, and which provides highly valued wood. Wood from this tree, used in cabinet making.

Watermelon. Annual plant (cucurbitaceous) cultivated in a warm climate, with prostrate stem, producing a large edible fruit, with very watery and refreshing pink flesh; the fruit itself.

Wheat. Cultivated annual plant (grass) whose grains are universally used for making flour and bread.

Yam. Food plant (dioscoreaceae) from tropical regions, with edible tuberous rhizomes, rich in starch. (Yams are twining, climbing lianas, grown on mounds with stakes; their tubers constitute an important part of the diet of tropical rural populations.) It is a perennial creeping food plant, especially cultivated in warm regions for its tuberous roots with a sweet taste; the tuber itself.

In spring, the season of flowers, the blossoming of the trees' leaves forming a sea of multicolored flowers, and adding to those of the natural ones, bring an inexpressible beauty to nature in celebration. All this made one think of the handling of a decorator who would rout any competitor. Indeed, who would ever dare to compete with the Decorator and the Architect of the universe?

Oh, another noteworthy fact! We weren't supposed to ignore the value of a piece of land around the world. Man attaches such importance to a piece of land that he prefers it to his fellow man, without thinking that the land belongs to God, and that he can claim it at any time. For the Bible tells us, in **Psalm 24:1:**

"To the Lord the earth and all that are in it. The world and those who inhabit it!"

How many human lives have been crucified trough the world for a piece of land or property. The striking example is the continual duel between Israel and Palestine, also called the Arab States. Before 1947, Palestine was a mixture of Jews and Arabs. In past years, bloody unrest pitted Palestinians against Jews.

To establish peace between the two antagonists, the U.N. (United Nations) decided to divide Palestine between a Jewish state and an Arab state. The Arabs (the Arabs or the Palestine's), refused to recognize Israel as an independent state. They refused to recognize that the earth belongs to God and he gives it to whomever he wanted to.

Thus, between 1948-1973, there were four Arab-Israeli wars. In the third war, also called the six-day war, in June 1967, the Arabs suffered an embarrassing defeat, and Israel took from them these following pieces of land: the West Bank, Gaza, the Golan and the Sinai. Since then, these territories occupied by Israel have been the scene of popular Arab uprisings. And for these pieces of land thousands and thousands of human lives have been sacrificed.

Where I grew up, and where the Lord chose me, setting me apart for his service, a mystery was revealed to me during the writing of this book. This secret is that the Lord has proved that he is the possessor of all that exists on earth; that he can gladly use it for the blessing of man whom he has created in his image and likeness.

O wonder! The Lord entered into private properties, divided the land, claimed a part of it for himself, and turned it into a spring of living, purified water that flowed directly from within ground.

Then, he offered it to all the people in the neighborhood and even to passers-by. At that time, I was about ten years old and already an avid bible reader. As I thought about it, it appeared in my mind like a sign placed on the entrance gate of the water sources where everyone came to draw, this verse in **Isaiah 55:1a:**

"All you who are thirsty, come to the waters, even the one who has no money!"

One of the most popular springs at the time was the running water spring of Débauché, a section of Limbé, in northern Haiti. Almost, and even all the people in my neighborhood and the surrounding had come to draw there, fresh water. They invaded this part of private property, and no one ever questioned them. I, too, benefited of this blessing of God's infinite love. For I went there to draw, without paying a penny.

At the entrance to this source, it is as if everyone and even the apparent owner of this piece of land read with admiration: here is the property of the Lord offered to all his children.

In groups, often with songs of joy, people of almost all strata: teenagers, youth and adults, formed a long line and went towards these springs which the Lord fenced as his private properties in the midst of private properties and filled their buckets with water.

What is this helpless voice that would advise me not to serve such a marvelous, incomparable God? Inhabitants or passers-by were amazed to observe the marvels of the Lord, to contemplate the infinite goodness of God?

The people of this neighborhood were very humble, and very selfless. They mutually shared their food and the products of their fields. For example, I used to accompany my father to the fields. We went on a horse or donkey. Back home, with the animal laden with foodstuff, he shared them with many other families.

The majority of the people around me were superstitious and adopted an evil angel as their protector. Yet these people were, more often than not, stricken with greater misfortunes than ordinary people. Because, the bad angels do not seek to protect, but to abuse and destroy.

Indeed, and it is certain, that the true protection is found in Jesus-Christ and only in Christ. These inhabitants were pure country people. They rarely went or participated in city activities.

Our church was erected in the town of Limbe, a town located in the north of Haiti. My parents very rarely went to church, but they did go quite often to an evangelical station not far from home, which they considered their church.

My father was a very hard-working farmer and a visionary trader. He proceeded to the purchase and resale of domestic animals: Oxen, pigs and goats. Sometimes he traveled long distances on foot or on horseback, fifteen to twenty kilometers a day. He would return home with one or two animals, covering an even longer distance, because very often these animals are slow or exhausted from traveling such a long distance. My father was very patient with them and gave them respite, at least every hour.

Quite often, he returned home later than he had hoped. He has played all the legal cards to offer his children a better life, while many other surrounding children are starving or have never had the opportunity to sit on a school desk. This is the main reason which pushed me to give him an even better living at the end of his life.

It was also impressive to see that he managed large sums of money, without a formal education. Furthermore, he didn't employ any accountant. In many circumstances he has told me the value of a sum of money; after checking I found exactly the value revealed.

Again I repeat my father didn't have the chance to receive a formal education, but he knew how to raise a happy, united and well-supported family. He used three days a week for his trade; the other four days were divided into two parts: a part for his personal activities and the other part, to meet the needs of the family and also to spend time with my mother and her three children: Adélucia, Edna and me, Morales.

Remember that my parents have accepted Christ since my childhood, but with no perseverance. Alleluia! The Lord got hold of me through a spiritual mentor; through natural and spiritual events, and through divine revelations.

In my district and the surrounding districts, there were thousands of inhabitants, the majority of whom were pagans, and a diviner considered himself king of the pagans. However, almost everyone lived as one family. All, including the diviner, were apparently protective of children and young people.

CHAPTER TEN
MY MENTOR

Among the people in my neighborhood, there were only about four Christian families, including mine. But, the most fervent and respected lady as a spiritual leader was called: Sister Nélia Bélizaire, nicknamed 'Aunt Née' by all the teenagers and young adults who knew her. It was she, O wonder, that the Lord chose to introduce to me this spiritual treasure that is the gospel.

How unthinkable it was that all children, teenagers and young country people, no matter what neighborhood or section they lived in, would call unknown or known adults: "Uncle or Aunt." An adult from the neighborhood or even elsewhere, was traditionally authorized, by the parents themselves, to correct, reprimand children, adolescents and even young adults, in the event that the latter had committed an offense or acted immorally.

They even had the right to spank them without opposition; and if time permitted, they would have taken these children to their parents who would have sincerely thanked them. Therefore, almost all rural societies in the country led a life almost completely free from violence. However; fetish, magic, divination and many other pernicious practices have poisoned, in a way, this happy atmosphere which would have promised such a pleasant country life. These practices have been used for so-called personal protection, but not primarily to attack and confuse other families.

'Aunt Née' lived not far from my house. Her husband and my father lived like two brothers. Over time, they became loyal partners in business affairs. She was a very pious woman. She was respected and honored by the entire neighborhood. She provided me with the same maternal affection as her own children. She once said to me, "I consider you my own son because of your good behavior and your fear of God.

Eternal recognition! She was the one who gave me the first notions of the gospel, led me to church and to prayer meetings. I owe her an unpayable debt.

The results of her devotion and piety shaped my spiritual life and made me who I am today: pastor, lecturer, teacher and writer. I will only mention two memorable results of his spiritual devotion that I witnessed myself. I have experienced two pagan festivities held in Haiti:

1. The *'Mardi Gras'* that gathered large musical processions, and rallied hundreds or thousands of people.

2. *The Rara'* which was the diminutive of *'Mardi Gras'*, was a small festivity organized at the local level, with drums and other small instruments.

FIRST RESULT FROM 'AUNT NEE' SPIRITUAL DEVOTION

I remember an interesting event that had happened, concerning the powerful diviner, mentioned above, and 'Aunt Née'. The diviner was the king of the district. But he always felt a great fear for 'Aunt Née'. He was the leader of the 'Rara' group in my neighborhood. He used this group specifically to raise funds, with the aim of furthering his divinatory practice. When this group was in action, it shook the

Entire neighborhood, because It was afraid of the diviner. He would gladly enter every family's yard, without warning, whether the owner was willing to receive him or not. After performing, each family had an obligation to contribute.

When this group was heading towards the home of 'Aunt Née', the diviner would warn: "Attention! We will not enter this woman's house. I have nothing to do with her. Never set foot in this woman's court". This proves that soothsayers, magicians and demons have testified that the power of God in the lives of faithful Christians is always greater than theirs.

SECOND RESULT FROM 'AUNT NEE' SPIRITUAL DEVOTION

One day 'Aunt Née' told me the story of God's great love for her, which I recognized as a reward for her great faith in his omnipotence.

She came from the big market. I want to remind readers that apart from the local market (Le marché de la commune du Limbé), its district was dotted with large markets, scattered in several distant places and on different days. Thus, the traders, classified as buyers, sellers and breeders, traveling from very far to go to the big market. They returned, quite often, to their house until the evening. We are not supposed to ignore that in the countryside, in the evening, for lack of electricity, darkness covers all the districts. There was a place called 'Demon's Quarter. It was there that 'Aunt Née' had to pass to go home. Her husband, whose faith was much weaker than hers, did not have the temerity to go meet her. So she had to walk through this demonic neighborhood on her own. Yet, we have learned that demons are still afraid of many people. As soon as she arrived at this crossroads, she was surrounded by demons.

Suddenly, she saw someone in front of her. He looked like an angel. In an instant, she didn't know where she was. She lost consciousness. When she opened her eyes, she saw herself in her courtyard. Her husband opened the door to receive her. She asked him, "How do you know I am here". He replied, "You knocked at the door, didn't you?" After telling him her story, they both concluded that she was rescued by the angel of the Lord, and that the angel himself knocked at the door.

These are the sure ways that the Lord used to get hold of me, and never to turn back. Oh, how marvelous is the omniscient God, who chose me from my mother's womb! Now, without a doubt, I've agreed with King David in his song of exaltation or **Psalms 139:15-18** :

"My body was not hidden before you,
When I was made in a secret place,
Woven in the depths of the earth.
When I was only a shapeless mass, your eyes saw me;
And on your book were all written
The days that were destined for me,
Before any of them existed.
How impenetrable are your thoughts,
O God! How great is the number!
If I count them, they are more numerous
than the grains of sand.
I wake up, and I'm still with you".

It is that woman of deep faith and great consecration whom the Lord has chosen to teach me the first notions of the almightiness of the one true God and has prepared me to confront, without fear, all trials of life. At the center of all these overwhelming experiences that I will have encountered, mysteriously, my love for this great faithful God, became more and more intense. He did for me, as he did for Moses, Joseph, Job, Peter and the three young Hebrews, etc.

CHAPTER ELEVEN
Divine Interventions

EVENTS OF PERSONAL EXPERIENCES
AND SPIRITUAL FINDINGS

1) I had a childhood friend called Luckner Bélizaire. We grew up together. But, by circumstance or by choice, we have occupied two opposite poles. I was a Christian; he was a pagan. We lived about a kilometer apart between us. Growing up, our friendship cooled, a bit, for two reasons: I was going to school; he wasn't. I loved the Lord; he was making fun of my God. But, since we grew up together, the childhood memories were so strong between us, that we remained, even so, two friends.

I was humble and gentle, and although very young, I was also a visionary and consistent in my decisions. I stayed that way all my life. He was very strong, very open, very fiery and very popular. He thought he was invincible. All this self-confidence was designed for the simple reason that his mom was a servant of several evil spirits, called 'Loas', it was said, very powerful. They had the power, we have heard, to bring to nothing all those who attacked their servants. All the young people around, myself included, called him 'Louk'. He called me 'Mora'. I used to say to him: 'Louk', my friend, give your life to Christ; **He is almighty!**

He is the only one who can protect you in all dangers. In presence of all the other young friends of different interests, he said: "Mora, my dear, Jesus cannot do anything for me. The doctrine called the gospel is a joke". He continued: "With all these Loas', my mother has more power than these two, combined: your Jesus and your gospel. Have you not witnessed, he added, that no disease, natural or supernatural, has ever had power over my mother's children? We are protected by his powerful 'Loas'! When we are attacked by the enemy or by another evil spirit; she called on her 'Loas' who had always come and immediately delivered us".

Statistics have reported, especially around the 1960s, that 85% of young Haitians did not have the opportunity to attend school. The other 15% are divided into two categories: approximately 10% discontinued before the certificate of primary studies; after the certificate or after a few years of secondary studies. The 5% who remained, had the opportunity to attain rhetoric or philosophy. I had the great blessing of continuing and finishing my studies, in the big city of Cap-Haitian, by the grace and the infinite love of the omnipotent God who chose a good-hearted cousin, having offered me this blessed opportunity.

On a Saturday, around three o'clock in the afternoon, being in Cap-Haitian, perched on a balcony and plunged myself in my study, I was suddenly distracted by someone of my acquaintance who closely observed my friendship with Luckner, ran up in haste next to me, and with great emotion, told me that my childhood friend was suddenly and seriously ill. His mom spent all day from Saturday until Sunday morning, invoking her 'Loas'. No answer! All of her 'Loas' were powerless to rescue him, and very early on Sunday morning Luckner breathed his last breath.

Neither his mother or her 'Loas' could not save him. The whole neighborhood was in motion for a young boy of about seventeen, so popular, so fiery, who had just disappeared like a breeze. In addition, all the young people in the neighborhood lived as one family. Everyone was surprised that this lady, servant of these powerful spirits, could not heal or save her son. It was later reported, according to the diagnosis of a diviner, that another more powerful group of evils spirits revolted against those whose his mother served. The more powerful ones won the victory. On the other hand, he pricked this young boy with his invisible prods.

Luckner began to shed blood like a flooded river, at midnight of that Saturday and Sunday at six o'clock in the morning he was already dead. What a lesson for those who walk without God or groping with God and who put their trust in the uncertain power of wicked spirits. For, God alone is omnipotent, omniscient and omnipresent. I blessed his holy and glorious name for having chosen me for one of his protégés since my early childhood.

In Haiti, almost every family or their ancestors served one or more bad angels, also called: bad spirits, evil spirits, wicked spirits or '*Loas*'. For them, these spirits are their invincible protectors, because two and even three families serve the same spirits. And it went from parents to parents or generation to generation. However, the claimed or a descendant can move away from it by conversion or a strong will.

Indeed, I met families who refused to serve an evil spirit. My father was an example quite striking. I never suspected my father, serving a Loa' or an evil spirit. I never knew the grandparents on my mother's side. But, I had the blessing of living with my grandparents on my father's side, during my childhood and my adolescence. I was told neither one had served the '*Loa*'.

I was already an adult when I lost them. They never offered anything to any '*Loa*'. However, those who served the '*Loas*' had the obligation to celebrate each year, a festival in their honor. This holiday was strictly observed lest the wicked master would become angry with them and destroy the whole family, by illness, a succession of calamities, or sudden death.

During this celebration, these families presented the following elements: money, oxen, goats, hens, etc. and all kinds of food products. The food prepared for the feast was a mixture of everything. It was then distributed profusely to each attendant, after presenting the best part to the so-called protective spirits or '*Loas*'.

At that time, the family in charge of the party chose one or more soothsayers to be masters of ceremonies. After all these seemingly joyful manifestations, these families became more miserable than ever.

I once heard this report of one such ceremony: It involved a family choosing two renowned soothsayers to be masters of ceremonies at a feast given in honor of their 'Loa'. It was reported that all day there was a discussion between them, because they could not agree on any decision, and this party became a total confusion. Nothing could be accomplished. The knowledge acquired from the teaching of my divine Master, Jesus of Nazareth, taught me that there was nothing astonishing in this matter.

Let us therefore listen to the Master in his teaching, recorded in **Matthew 12:25-26:**
"Every kingdom divided against itself is devastated, and every city or house divided against itself cannot stand. If Satan drives out Satan, he is divided against himself; how then shall his kingdom stand?"

I learned and witnessed that on my mother's side, some family members serve these kinds of 'Loas.' But, God be praised, on my father's side, we never mentioned these kinds of practices. I also observed that no relatives on my father's side served these evil spirits. God who chose me from my mother's womb, raised me among my father's relatives, and I never participated in these pernicious practices. These practices were not only popular among the country people, but among almost all Haitian families, regardless of their intellectual or financial position. Thus, the Lord developed in me, from my young age, a disgust for these superstitions.

2) I had a classmate, called Maniphart Moralien. We did all our primary education together. When we were in certificate class, our school needed repairs and we had to be moved to another facility three hours walk from my house and two hours walk from my classmate's house. Since it was very difficult to get us home after school, our school principal, who was very attached to me, and who was also a good-hearted christian, made arrangements for us to stay in a dormitory at the school interior.

My friend's mom brought us food twice a day. She also assured me that there was no difference between me and her son. She told me that she considered us two sons of her notches. Since then, Maniphart and I lived like two brothers and a filial love was also formed in my heart for her. I treated this lady like my own mother the rest of her life. However, a great abyss separated us: I was a christian, Maniphart and his parents were pagans. I did all I could to win them for Christ, but in vain. The main reason for my failure is that I was still a teenager, and teenagers at that time had no influence on adults, as well as young people of his age who had become lost in their philosophy. The main point of this story is that when the final exams of primary studies were near, my friend approached and told me: my dear Mora (His nickname for me), my parents were going to consult a diviner to ensure my success. I encourage you to ask your parents to do the same for you. Otherwise, you know what will happen! You will definitely be failed! I answered him with an emotional gesture and with all my composure: Maniphart, my friend, don't you know that I am a christian and I have always behaved as such before you during the whole time of our friendship? All my faith has rested on Christ and Christ alone. He is the Almighty God, the God of heaven and earth. It was in him that I put all my trust. Hear Him in **Isaiah 45:20-23:**

"Assemble and come,
approach together, survivors of nations!
They have no intelligence, those who carry their wooden idol,
And who invoke a god unable to save.
Declare it, and make them come!
Let them take advice from each other!
Who foretold these things from the beginning,
And long announced them?
Am I not the Lord? There is no other God but me,
I am the only just and saving God. Turn to me,
and you will be saved,
All of you who are at the ends of the earth!
For I am God, and there is no other.
I swear by myself,

The truth comes out of my mouth and my word will not be revoked:
Every knee will bow before me,
Every tongue will swear by me".

Surprise! Surprise! Surprise!

According to the results of the exams, I was laureate in all the rural schools and my classmate who was going to ensure easy success and warned me of certain failure if I did not follow his path, was himself on the verge of failure. I associate my voice with David to exclaim in **Psalm 34:1:**

"I will bless the Lord at all times. His praise will always be in my mouth".

3) The United States has been considered a country where milk and honey flow. People from everywhere eagerly take refuge there, in search of fortune or well-being. Around the 1980s, a group of students and professors made a firm decision to take advantage of a favorable opportunity to enter the United States.

For this, they have put everything under their feet, to enter this promised land. Thinking of all the goods I have done to them, to their community and the general appreciation I received from my beneficiaries, they felt the great joy of inviting me to leave with them. I embraced this kind and unexpected invitation with great appreciation.

Without wasting time, I gathered all the formalities and, we were ready to leave. Although I was the only christian in the group, I asked them to meet me in a designated place to claim God's providence. After this prayer addressed to the Supreme God, they asked to present a prayer to their god or their protective spirit. I had opposed this proposal adamantly, teaching them that there is only one true God; it is to this God that we must address our requests and supplications. Anyway, they insisted and decided to present their request to their imaginary gods. I refused to participate, and I asked them wisely to excuse me until after their prayer.

O power! Among a group of about eight people, I was the only one traveling at that time. Everyone should know that the God of sincere christians is the only true God. I was sincerely saddened, in that, the whole group that invited me was blocked for one reason or another. But, I blessed the name of God for his infinite wisdom, his omnipotence and his faithfulness.

I remembered, in this case, the words of Job, extolling the almightiness and the infinite wisdom of God, in **Job 12:13-16:**
"In God resides wisdom and power.
Advice and intelligence belong to him.
What he knocks down will not be open
He whom it imprisons will not be delivered.
It retains the waters and everything dries up;
He loses them, and the earth is devastated.
He possesses strength and prudence;
He masters the one who goes astray
or lead others astray".

On the second Saturday of October, that is October 13, 1990, I woke up very early, to prepare myself to begin my activities of the day. First of all, I knelt at the feet of the Lord, to ask him to guide me.

After a good shower, I had my breakfast. Now I was ready to tackle 'number one' of my itinerary:

THE ALLIANCE OF THE HAITIAN BAPTIST CHURCHES
INFORMATIVE MEETING

This meeting was to take place in Jersey City, New Jersey. The time for my departure had arrived. I took my notebook, my bible, my song book, and I said bye, bye to my tender wife, with a gentle kiss.

I then took the direction of the door to exit. As I opened the door, I heard a phone call. I felt a little disturbed, and I hadn't wanted to take the phone off, because I don't like to miss my appointments, and I like to always be on time in everything I do. So I wanted to be on time for the meeting in question. However, my intuition or the Holy Spirit, I assumed, commanded me to answer the call, before leaving. I shyly took the phone off and said hello! A sincere and faithful sister of the church that I led, then Sister Annette Prévilon, cried out with great emotion: "Pastor Morales! Pastor Morales! Issue! Issue!" As if this beloved sister was going to tell me of the sudden death of a member of the church. I told her: do not worry, beloved! Calm down! The Lord is on our side and I'm coming right away.

Now tell me what happened! "The waters have invaded the church," was her urgent and disturbing news.

Don't worry! Preferably, start praying, I told her.

I want to mention to readers that the church mentioned above was the EBen-Ezer Haitian Baptist Church of Westbury, Long Island, New York, where I was founder and pastor. Without emotion and with great calm, I said to her: do not worry, beloved sister! Calm down, I'm coming right away. Don't worry! Preferably, start praying.

I called one of the leaders of the Alliance to explain my absence. Then I called one of my church workers. I asked him to call a plumbing company without delay. For we have a problem in the church toilet. He let me know that on Saturday in Westbury almost all the companies closed their doors. I told him okay! I'm coming. I took my boots and a few spare clothes. I decided to set off in the direction of Westbury, Long Island, New York.

Now, I would advise my readers to pay close attention to the sequel to this both pathetic and glorious story. Indeed, there will be much to learn for an abundant and faith-fortified christian life. Arrived at the church, my hand was unconsciously thrown over my mouth and head. The temple looked like a crossing of a flooded river, and no one was there to help. The sister who called me had to leave to fulfill a pressing obligation. She was just passing by to take a look at the church temple, before going about her personal business. The temple was completely flooded with the pompous waters from the toilet. The church was still young and weak. I had only a handful of workers there and none of them came to my aid, as if the church was my personal property. I tried to contact several cleaning and plumbing companies, no one answered me. It was a test from the Lord; he had a plan for me, and he was going to burst his glory into my life, after an unbearable ordeal. During time of trials, the Lord has always given faithful christians the strength to endure. Sometimes in the middle and especially at the end of our sufferings, he made his glory shine in our life. Let's see, in a way, what the bible said about:

1 Corinthians 10:13:
"No temptation has seized you except what is common to man. And God is faithful; he will not let you be tempted beyond what you can bear. But when you are tempted, he will also provide a way out so that you can stand up under it."

The story continues. I took off my shepherd's clothes to put on spare clothes, work clothes; I put on my boots and gloves. I took a washing and drying machine. I courageously set to work. The more I dried, the more the waters pumped out of the toilet, and at regular intervals. I started to dry exactly at noon. After three hours of cleaning and drying, or about three in the afternoon, nothing changed.

I tried my best to stop the water pumping, but to no avail. Meanwhile, my mind and body began to be weary, and I implored, weeping: Lord, strengthen me, for there must be service tomorrow, for the glory of your name.

Meanwhile, a so-called worker, a member of the executive committee of the church, appeared. A feeling of relief eased my heart, at the thought that he had come, no doubt, to offer me his help. But, to my spiritual and moral disappointment, he said to me: "Uh!!! Pastor Morales, you have the gall to work in such a condition. I'm sorry, I can't help you, and he's gone".

Then, I felt a sword sever my heart, piece by piece. I regained my strength and told him when he was leaving: you can't help me, can you? Me, I am ready to accept everything for Christ who gave himself as a sacrifice, to pay the price for my sins.

"Good luck, pastor." Those were his goodbye words. These ruthless actions tore my heart. But, I ended up realizing that God wanted it that way. He wanted me to face these trials. For this faithful and mysterious God was going to reveal himself to me, with power.

Immediately after the indifferent worker left, the spirit of discouragement dissipated within me, and a sudden strength entered my whole being. I gave a loud cry of relief, in the form of a prayer, with these words of deep gratitude and tears of satisfaction in my eyes: "Lord Jesus, you, King of kings, perfect God, you have left your heavenly throne, your eternal throne, to come down to this land of sin, to take birth in a stable, the place most despised, least frequented, even by the poorest people, to prepare yourself to be crucified on the bloody cross at Golgotha, to pay the price for my sins, for my iniquities. I love you, God of great mercy; I am grateful to you, my God, my King, and I want to suffer for you. I only ask you to come to my aid. Strengthen me in this situation which, humanly seemed impossible to me.

Redoubled in strength, I went back to work, and I still continued to dry with no result. At five o'clock in the afternoon, a so-called woman of prayer from the church had come and struck me with another thunderbolt: "Pastor Morales. That's enough! Tell the church members that there will be no service tomorrow." I have it answered with unexpected passion: sister, go tell all the members of the church that there will be a solemn service tomorrow, in honor of our God, and for their blessings; invite friends and neighbors I continued. She answered me with a disdainful nod: "Okay, pastor! I can't stay any longer", as if she took me for a madman, a visionary and left.

My young wife, then with two small children, called me several times during the day and was very sad that no one had come to my aid. I comforted her with these words of consolation: don't you worry, darling; I did everything for the glory of God, and he will not abandon me.

I didn't live in Westbury; even when I couldn't find a plumbing company, the church workers who lived there would have tried to find a plumber or someone with some knowledge of plumbing to help with the situation. Everyone showed a cold heart. It's like if the LORD has hardened the hearts of all, because he will himself come in power to help me.

My wife called me again at ten o'clock at night, and said: "My love (My darling, my love); where are you?" I replied, like nothing was: I am still in the temple. She lamented:" I beg you; come now. I won't sleep until you come. So tell me what happened?" Don't worry, I replied to her? I have to prepare the temple for service tomorrow, God willing. Go and sleep in peace; I'm coming. Let not your heart be troubled, our God is faithful. He will never leave us.

During this time, the waters, coming from the toilet, continued to pump with more intensity. At eleven o'clock at night, when I saw no way to stop this mysterious water pumping, I called my wife, to tell her: honey, the work is not finished yet. Pray and go to sleep, I beg you. The Lord is with me. She was starting to cry and reiterated, "I'm not going to sleep until you come." At that time, she had two babies. I reminded her Do this for Jesus. Put your trust in him; pray and go to sleep. She now has obeyed. I closed the phone with these words: the Lord is with us.

Undeterred, I continued to dry, singing and glorifying the Lord until 11:45 p.m. to no avail. Then, my strength was completely exhausted. I threw myself belly against the floor, on the podium of the church, and I began to pray like this: Lord, are you going to let me spend twelve hours of time, working tirelessly, to accomplish nothing? Are you going to close the doors of the Church tomorrow? Do you know that the weak and the enemies of the faith will say: "He spent all his time in church last night, to show that he has a lot of faith and that he loves the Lord more than all others, but he accomplished nothing".

No Lord, it cannot be, and never will be, while I give myself up to sacrifice purely and simply in recognition of your many blessings to me.

Lord, surely you heard when I told the sister, while she told me to close the church's doors tomorrow , to go tell christians and non-christians , to come in big numbers at the church, tomorrow.

Did I say it by pride or power? No! You are God. You know very well that I did it for your glory and your honor.

During this time, a dissembling sleep robbed me. Meanwhile, someone came to shake me and said: didn't you hear that your wife called you many times? I woke up with a start. No noise was heard. Stunned, I did not understand anything. After recognizing myself a little, I looked around me and around the church trembling, thinking that the pumping of water continued its course. The flow of water ceased. Everything was silent around me. I couldn't have believed my eyes and my ears. I was completely exhausted, and I felt a void within me. I thought I was still between sleep and wakefulness. I shook my head to make sure I was really awake; still no noise. The water pumping had completely stopped. I was like crazy and exclaimed: thank you, Lord! Thank you, Lord! How great you are! How powerful you are! Your mercy goes from generation to generation, and I added like those who received your revelations: who are like you, on earth and in heaven?

I went back to work, with this song of gratitude: "In heaven and on earth, there is no name so great..." I dried, washed and disinfected the entire sanctuary. I then called my wife to give her the good news, and she rejoiced and glorified this great God of mercy. I took over the road, singing, dancing, glorifying the God eternally powerful and merciful. I had arrived to my house at two o'clock in the morning, and my wife was waiting for me at the door. She surrounded me with her delicate arms, telling me: "you are truly the son of Abraham and together we bless the name of God".

The next day, as planned, we had a spectacular service in honor of our God. Let us be grateful to this mighty and wonderful God for his goodness to us. Let us love the Lord with all our heart. Let us have sublime faith in this real and almighty God. And so we will have the grace to benefit from his wonders and miracles.

MY ILLNESS AND MY MIRACULOUS CURE

I often heard, by hearsay, and during my adolescence, that in Haiti, certain neighbors, people from the same neighborhood or the surroundings, classmates often felt jealous of intelligent students, and sometimes even sought to eliminate them.

By the grace of God, I was among the brightest of my classmates. God graced me with great faith and I never felt like anyone could hurt me. After the tenth grade exams, I was admirably admitted to Rheto or eleventh grade. It was really a celebration, a real joy for my parents and apparently even for some neighbors of great humility. To reach this school grade in Haiti, indeed, was a great hope for the parents who count, quite often, in the support of their children reaching a place in the high society.

During this summer holidays I was rejoicing of my success of that same year, I had fallen seriously ill. After a week, the illness was getting more and more serious. I could neither eat nor drink. It is not meant to ignore that the gods of non-christian Haitians were the soothsays or fortune tellers. And besides, at that time, my parents were not as firm in faith as I was. But, blessed be the Lord, my father always abhorred these gods. He did not believe their predictions, and deliberated openly against them. All my father's friends encouraged him to visit a diviner on my behalf, especially my late aunt, Lucilia Saintilus, who loved me like her own son and whom I too loved like my own mother. During my illness, that terrified my parents, my neighbors and my close friends, my aunt, who lived not far from me, visited me day and night. It seems that at night she didn't even bother to look at the clock. Quite often, she had come, either at midnight, one o'clock, two o'clock, three o'clock in the morning, etc. One day, she came to meet my father at three o'clock in the morning and said to him: Magot (my father's family nickname), don't you see that the criminals are trying to remove Momo (my family nickname) from your hands? Do not forget, she added, that you have only one boy who, by his respect, his intelligence and his progress, has already brought honor to the family. I advise you to go visit a diviner to save 'Momo' and I'm determined to go with you.

Could anyone believe it? During this moving and frightening conversation, they thought I was sleeping. I was quite awake, however, and in excruciating pain. Incredible, but true, the Lord gave me the courage to remain silent throughout the conversation. Now, after my aunt left, I called my father who was as humble as a child, and I said to him: 'Magot' (That's what all his children called him too), I heard everything that was said. I know my aunt loves me very much, but she's not a Christian.

'Magot', I continued, listen to your son who loves and honors you. Don't listen to my aunt and don't consult a medium for me. For he Lord, my God, has the power to heal me, and I continued: if you do not listen to me and go to a diviner for me, I will die and I will go straight to my heavenly Father, and you, you will lose me forever. To my great surprise, my father hugged me with both arms around my neck and said to me, with the humility of a child and with streams of tears running down his face: "My son, it will be done according to your will. I guarantee you that I will place your illness in the hands of the great Master ". I cried:

    Hallelujah!
    And we embraced each other again with tears of joy.

In the evening, o wonder, the angel of the Lord approached me and said: you are cured. However, the next day I became more ill and so ill that I could not stand. They rushed me to Bon Samaritain hospital in Limbé. Upon arriving there, all the rooms were then occupied. Doctors checked me out and sent me back home as to say: the case is already lost.

When I arrived home, my parents were crying inconsolably, as if I were already dead. In the midst of my desolation and in my bitter suffering, I was convinced that my God had already healed me.

I blindly believed in his great fidelity and his irrevocable promises. I called my father and I said to him: console yourself 'Magot' (papa), and go and tell the others to console themselves. For the angel of the Lord appeared to me last night and told me that I was healed. And, my father responded, again like a child: okay, "Okay, my son", shaking his head in obedience, at the thought that I tried to use some means to console him. But, his desperation was stronger than his obedience. In other words, he had endeavored to obey, since the great concern was plainly on his face. The next day, at dawn in the morning, I felt a force circulating within me. I got up and stood on my own two feet. Since then, I was completely cured. I want to reiterate to all Christians, and to my readers, that when scientists and scholars lament: "End stop"; the Lord contradicts them with: "Period at the line".

This is why I am the way I am: humble servant of God, and I want to be so all my life.

This is why I am the way I am: loving God and urged on by his love.

That's why I am the way I am: compassionate, and always seeking to help the poor and disinherited.

Who wouldn't be, after having made acquaintance with a God so great, so rich in goodness and mercy?

Who wouldn't be, after learning that such a powerful Jesus, this 'God made man' and 'God with us', was born in the dwelling of animals, called manger ; he who created heaven and earth with everything they contain, and later accepted an ignominious death, a shameful death to pay the price for our sins, our iniquities? That's what he said, by the pen of the prophet Isaiah, in **Isaiah 53:5:**

"*He was wounded for our sins,*
Broken for our iniquities; The chastisement that gives us peace fell on him,
And it is by his stripes that we are healed ".

From thousands and one actions he granted me the grace to perform, to glorify his name, I remember that in March 1979, I went to a restaurant and ate my fill. This restaurant was placed at the corner of a public square. After this hearty meal, I headed to the public square for a siesta. There, I saw several poor people, dying of hunger; asking for alms with a hopeless air and tone, devoid of any hope of living. Their faces were anguished, suggesting that life did not exist for them. Instantly, my heart was deeply touched with compassion. I heard a voice, saying to me: "What are you doing thinking, reflecting and being touched with compassion? Your belly is full and your pocket has surplice money, right? Feed them! For they too are my children, created in my image and likeness.

I immediately sprang into action with a face wet with tears of compassion. I had enough in my pocket to give them enough to buy a cup of pistachios and a piece of cassava. After that, every time I had to go to a restaurant, I took a poor man with me and we ate at the same table. Also, I visited them from time to time and became their friend.

I updated this testimony, to remind the privileged that their privileges come from God and that they must not close their eyes and their hearts to the hungry and the unfortunate. The wishes for blessings received from these poor people were numerous and sincere enough to give me a long and prolonged life.

Satan, jealous of the gifts and blessings received from God, waged war against me, to exterminate me and keep me miserable, by enormous losses, calamities and afflictions of all kinds. But, who can shut the floodgates of heaven against the chosen servants of God, who struggle on their knees to do his will? The faithful and merciful God assured me: "I, the Lord, will open the floodgates of heaven and will bless you abundantly in order to proclaim my name and continue this work of charity to which I have called you and which is so pleasing to me".

Gifted with a godly intelligence and instructed by one of the most eminent principals and teachers of primary schools, teacher Marcel Toussaint, I was the brightest of my classmates. Taking advantage of this instruction well done, I was the winner, after the final examinations of primary studies on all the rural schools. I myself was not aware of these laurels, because I was in the countryside and had no access to radio. But God, who knows how to choose the humble, the most desperate, to make them trusted servants and place them among the great and even at the head of the great, has raised me up, a benefactor, a good-hearted cousin, Director Wilson Saintilus, a man of renown and great learning.

He was one of the firstborn of my generation and took a great interest in the intellectual development of many young people, especially his parents. He was the first to hear of my successes in the official primary school certificate exams through radio. Despite this great success, and the good will of my father, he was not fortunate enough to send me even to the town of Limbé, commercial center of the commune of Limbé, let alone to the big city of Cap-Haitien or Port-au-Prince, the capital of Haiti.

But God, who has already planned everything for his servant before the exams, chose a good-hearted cousin who became like a brother, to take care of my secondary studies, which would be impossible for me without him.

Indeed, he loved his close relatives very much. Still, he and I didn't really have a close relationship, since he was a city dweller and I, a country man. Moreover, he was my senior by several years, by ten years, to be precise. However, with pomp of joy, he sent for me from the countryside, to enter Cap-Haitien, the big city in the North. There, he took responsibility for my secondary education and enrolled me, without delay, at the Lycée Philippe Guerrier in Cap-Haitien, where I took the admission exams and passed without hassle. There too we lived together for many years in a good fraternal relationship. I owe him eternal gratitude. To my God himself, I owe him my life.

Now the moment of great interest has arrived. Now is the time to pay more attention, because I am going to present the picture of the first great miracle that the Lord performed in my life, not by revelation or vision, but on waking and with the naked eye.

So let's start! Alright! Let's go! Saturday April 22, 1972, while living with Director Wilson Saintilus in Cap-Haitien, he gave me a $20.00 US bill to make him some purchases. Twenty American dollar, in those days, had great value. As a young person, I felt honored and I placed, in all confidence, this note in the bottom of my pocket. From my house to the store, I had to cover a distance of twenty kilometers on foot. Arriving there and before starting shopping, I penetrated my hand in my pocket, to make sure the money was ready. O misfortune, my pocket was empty and those twenty dollars were gone! I searched my pocket with noise and mad anxiety, no money! I do not need to describe the trouble in my heart, in this annoying circumstance. Let's not forget that I had to travel a distance of 30 minutes to return home, and the way back was strewn with passers-by. Anyone who saw this $20.00 note would be eager to remove it secretly and with great satisfaction. It would be a godsend for that person. I was returning, panting, and shedding streams of tears, with no hope of finding that money. I was an honest teenager with a sense of responsibility. I lamented: Lord my God, you alone know my heart. You know the $20.00 is gone, but the rest of the world will think I'm a liar and a thief. Save me from my distress, O Lord my God, and give me this $20.00, for your faithfulness and great mercy. After about twenty minutes of running, at full speed, desperate and wet with sweat, behind a barracks, not far from my home, something hit me on my chest. At first glance, I thought it was a butterfly or a dry tree leaf that the wind blew away. I lowered my head and watched fearfully. O happiness, the $20.00 bill was slapped on my chest. I threw myself on my knees to exclaim: infinitely good and omnipresent and omniscient God, who can, like you, save an unfortunate like me from this great affliction? I love you, o Lord, my God. Help me serve you faithfully the rest of my life.

Sunday January 12, 1964 was the happiest day of my life. It was the day I was officially admitted among God's chosen ones. This Sunday at one o'clock in the afternoon, while I slept alone under the coolness of the trees in a family resting place, a few steps from the house, someone with the majesty of an angel, appeared to my bedside and said to me: "The Lord has chosen you among your people and you belong to him. When I woke up, I danced, I jumped for joy before the incredibly holy, incredibly good God, and I cried out with great joy, with these words:

"Thank you Lord!
Thank you Lord!
Unworthy that I am,
You chose me among your beloved children.
I was a child, because then I was only eleven years old,
When you chose me".

A year later, I started preaching the gospel. Satan who was jealous of the honor I received from the Most High, sent his emissaries to destroy me, and the Lord had come immediately to my help. On Saturday, January 22, 1965, while I was sleeping, I saw a group of wicked soldiers running after me to take my life away. I hurried hastily. When I arrived in the middle of a bush, filled with the Holy Spirit, I stood like a mighty warrior, invincible and dispelled of all fear. In the blink of an eye, I was surrounded by these furious soldiers who each carried murderous weapons around their loins, whose leader looked like Goliath. I had absolutely nothing in my hand. While they were going to raise their arms to kill me, I heard a voice saying to me:

Lower your head and use what you see. I looked down and saw a small penknife, lying beside my feet. I grabbed it and hacked all the soldiers to pieces including their giant leader. I reasoned, at the end: Lord, you have really chosen me and you have armed me with power. My lips will glorify you forever.

It is an undeniable fact that the Lord manifests his power in sleep and in awakening to protect his servants who love him and who seek him with all their heart. I am one of the most striking examples. He placed in me a supernatural resistance against the deceptive tactics of the devil. He struck me with a thousand deadly arrows. He never could have struck me down by the power of God. This is why, my love for my God, has only increased, and this, since my tender childhood.

This vision that, everyone lives in mutual love, respect and protection, lit in my heart like a torch, like a consuming fire, and with the passage of time it only grew wider. Despite all the betrayals of the brothers whom I have so tenderly loved: young people, adults, old people, within the church of which I am the founder, the friendly churches, and even in my entourage; I cannot help forgiving them, loving them and thinking of their well-being.

I want repentance, but not vengeance; I want peace, but not war; I want love, but not hate, and I want God's blessing for everyone. That is why he strengthened me with divine revelations, through visions and by his own presence. For this fact and as he ordered me, I dedicate my life, to write and tell his wonders the rest of my life.

THE PANORAMA OF TWO UNITED FAMILIES

The Saintilus family and the Bélizaire family lived as one family although they lived in their respective homes. The two houses were within walking distance of each other. The Saintilus family had for ancestors: Fadéus and Talicia Saintilus and the Bélizaire family; Danus and Nélia Bélizaire, alias 'Aunt Née' whom God also chose for my spiritual mentor. The lives of three young people in these families and the providence of God will teach, to all humble hearts, the difference between those who wholeheartedly seek the presence of God and those who refuse to give their hearts to him. The three youngsters are: Brunice Bélizaire, Moralès Saintilus and Bernadin Bélizaire.

Brunice and Bernadin were blood brothers; and I, a close neighbor. However, we lived as three brothers. Brunice was my eldest and I was the eldest of Bernadin. Brunice was a little self-centered. He loved his family. But, he didn't have the ability to exteriorize it, especially to his father who brought me complaints against him, about his self-centered behevior. He was a little proud of himself and was very intelligent.

We grew up together for much of our lives, but we were never close friends when we were kids. Besides, her mother had two boys: Bernadin and Brunice whom she treated like two princes. I was younger than Brunice and didn't have that privilege he enjoyed. The fact is my parents were very humble with few resources.

'Aunt Née' was a devout servant of God and a successful Businesswoman respected by the whole community. Brunice and Bernadin were like the apple of her eyes, although she had other children. Brunice became an eminent teacher and disregarded the things of God. Bernadin chose his mother's God and served him zealously. Let it be remembered that it was this 'Aunt Nee' that God chose to be my spiritual mentor, and because of her love for God and for me, I became a slave of Jesus Christ and, I consecrated my whole body, my heart and my soul to serve my God. This christian lady, Nélia Bélizaire, known as *Aunt Née*, will remain in my heart as an indelible design for the rest of my life. Brunice was struck several times by fiery arrows from the evil one. His mother and the Christian family prayed earnestly and he was healed. For God accepted their requests and came to his aid. Despite everything, he had never devoted himself to God wholeheartedly. I told him, on many occasions: Brunice, my friend and brother, it's time to get serious with the gospel. Don't be stubborn. You have a spiritual treasure in your home, your mom, this woman who is faithful and devoted to her God.

You have been visited many times by death, but God has heard her prayer. Do not rely only on your mom's prayers. Remember everyone will individually answer to the judgment throne of God. Keep in mind that John the Baptist rebuked the Pharisees and Sadducees who, coming to his baptism, wore a spiritual covering, but inside, they were whitewashed tombs, ravenous wolves. He warns them to produce fruits worthy of repentance, instead of claiming that because of Abraham, their father and friend of God, no matter how sinful they may be, they will always be protected by divine power,

God is not only a God of mercy, but also a God of wrath and a consuming fire. When he punishes, the earth quakes and the unrepentant mourn. Brunice again turned a deaf ear to my salutary advice. Bernadin and I were also struck by the fiery arrows of Satan, but we repeated together: We will not die, we will live and we will recount the glory of the Lord.

O infinite graces! O faithfulness of God! Bernadin and I both became pastors and anointed of the Lord. But, oh sadness! O regret! My friend and brother Brunice Bélizaire was stricken with a last illness which took him to the afterlife, with all the amalgam of his knowledge at a very young or premature age. What lessons for the unbelievers and those who walk hobbled in God's way!

However, it is not yet too late. God, in his mercy stretches out the two hands of a shepherd, crying: "Come back to the green pasture. Today is the day of salvation; today is the day of grace!"

CHAPTER TWELVE
Tributes and Recognition

A fter reviewing all the wonders of the Lord in my life, I was immersed in the labyrinth of unlimited gratitude and I exclaimed loudly: Lord, my God, give me the grace to add my song of gratitude to those of your holy servants, among others: Moses, Deborah, Hannah, Mary, Zechariah, David.

MOSES

Considering his salvation from the waters, in the protective basket; his position as prince of the land of Egypt; his mighty staff; the ten plagues; eyewitnesses to the result of his immaculate faith in the parting of the Red Sea into walls of water right and left, where the people of Israel crossed dry-footed and with outstretched arms, and the return of the waters to terrify Pharaoh and swallow up his horsemen, his chariots fiercely pursued the people of God, Moses and the children of Israel presented this song of gratitude, ready to burst from his heart, towards his God, the only true God, the king of kings, the absolute Master on earth, as it is heaven. Then Moses and the children of Israel sang this song to the Lord.

SONG OF MOSES EXODUS 15:1-19

I will sing to the Lord,
For He has triumphed gloriously!
The horse and its rider
He has thrown into the sea!

The Lord is my strength and song,
And He has become my salvation;
He is my God, and I will praise Him;
My father's God, and I will exalt Him.

The Lord is a man of war;
The Lord is His name.

Pharaoh's chariots and his army He has cast into the sea;
His chosen captains also are drowned in the Red Sea.

The depths have covered them;
They sank to the bottom like a stone.

Your right hand, O Lord, has become glorious in power;
Your right hand, O Lord, has dashed the enemy in pieces.

And in the greatness of Your excellence
You have overthrown those who rose against You;
You sent forth Your wrath;
It consumed them like stubble.

And with the blast of Your nostrils
The waters were gathered together;
The floods stood upright like a heap;
The depths congealed in the heart of the sea.

The enemy said, 'I will pursue,
I will overtake,
I will divide the spoil;

My desire shall be satisfied on them.
I will draw my sword,
My hand shall destroy them.'

You blew with Your wind,
The sea covered them;
They sank like lead in the mighty waters.

Who is like You, O Lord, among the gods?
Who is like You, glorious in holiness,
Fearful in praises, doing wonders?

You stretched out Your right hand;
The earth swallowed them.

You in Your mercy have led forth
The people whom You have redeemed;
You have guided them in Your strength
To Your holy habitation.

The people will hear and be afraid;
Sorrow will take hold of the inhabitants of Philistia.

Then the chiefs of Edom will be dismayed;
The mighty men of Moab,
Trembling will take hold of them;
All the inhabitants of Canaan will melt away.

Fear and dread will fall on them;
By the greatness of Your arm
They will be as still as a stone,
Till Your people pass over, O Lord,
Till the people pass over
Whom You have purchased.

You will bring them in and plant them
In the mountain of Your inheritance,

In the place, O Lord, which You have made
For Your own dwelling,
The sanctuary, O Lord, which Your hands have established.

The Lord shall reign forever and ever.

For the horses of Pharaoh went with his chariots and his horsemen into the sea, and the Lord brought back the waters of the sea upon them. But the children of Israel went on dry land in the midst of the sea.

DEBORAH

Deborah was a prophetess and a judge in Israel. The Lord used her to exterminate Jabin, king of the Canaanites, and Sisera, chief of his army, and their allies who, with their nine hundred chariots of iron, oppressed with violence the children of Israel, and this, since twenty years. The Israelite Barak, intrepid warrior, by order of Deborah, marched against Jabin and Sisera, oppressors of the children of Israel. Deborah addressed Barak as follows: "Isn't that the order given the Lord? Go, go to Mount Tabor, and take with you ten thousand men from the children of Naphthalia and from the inhabitants of Zebulun. I will draw Sisera, commander of the army of Jabin, with his chariots and his troops to you at the Kison Stream, and I will deliver him into your hands". And after ten thousand men the LORD routed Barak with the edge of the sword, Sisera, and all his chariots, and all the field, not sparing Jabin their king.

After this brilliant victory achieved only by the intervention of the power of the right hand of the Lord, Débora let flow from her heart waves of gratitude with a hymn that filled her heart to overflowing.

SONG OF DEBORA JUDGES: 5:1-31

When leaders lead in Israel,
When the people willingly offer themselves,

Bless the Lord!

Hear, O kings! Give ear, O princes!
I, even I, will sing to the Lord;
I will sing praise to the Lord God of Israel.

Lord, when You went out from Seir,
When You marched from the field of Edom,
The earth trembled and the heavens poured,
The clouds also poured water;

The mountains gushed before the Lord,
This Sinai, before the Lord God of Israel.

In the days of Shamgar, son of Anath,
In the days of Jael,
The highways were deserted,
And the travelers walked along the byways.

Village life ceased, it ceased in Israel,
Until I, Deborah, arose,
Arose a mother in Israel.

They chose new gods;
Then there was war in the gates;
Not a shield or spear was seen among forty thousand in Israel.

My heart is with the rulers of Israel
Who offered themselves willingly with the people.
Bless the Lord!

Speak, you who ride on white donkeys,
Who sit in judges' attire,
And who walk along the road.

Far from the noise of the archers, among the watering places,
There they shall recount the righteous acts of the Lord,
The righteous acts for His villagers in Israel;
Then the people of the Lord shall go down to the gates.

Awake, awake, Deborah!
Awake, awake, sing a song!
Arise, Barak, and lead your captives away,
O son of Abinoam!

Then the survivors came down, the people against the nobles;
The Lord came down for me against the mighty.

From Ephraim were those whose roots were in Amalek.
After you, Benjamin, with your peoples,
From Machir rulers came down,
And from Zebulun those who bear the recruiter's staff.

And the princes of Issachar were with Deborah;
As Issachar, so was Barak
Sent into the valley under his command;
Among the divisions of Reuben
There were great resolves of heart.

Why did you sit among the sheepfolds,
To hear the pipings for the flocks?
The divisions of Reuben have great searching of heart.

Gilead stayed beyond the Jordan,
And why did Dan remain on ships?
Asher continued at the seashore,
And stayed by his inlets.

Zebulun is a people who jeopardized their lives to the point of death,
Naphtali also, on the heights of the battlefield.

The kings came and fought,
Then the kings of Canaan fought

In Taanach, by the waters of Megiddo;
They took no spoils of silver.

They fought from the heavens;
The stars from their courses fought against Sisera.

The torrent of Kishon swept them away,
That ancient torrent, the torrent of Kishon.
O my soul, march on in strength!

Then the horses' hooves pounded,
The galloping, galloping of his steeds.

'Curse Meroz,' said the 7angel of the Lord,
'Curse its inhabitants bitterly,
Because they did not come to the help of the Lord,
To the help of the Lord against the mighty.'

Most blessed among women is Jael,
The wife of Heber the Kenite;

Blessed is she among women in tents.

He asked for water, she gave milk;
She brought out cream in a lordly bowl.

She stretched her hand to the tent peg,
Her right hand to the workmen's hammer;
She pounded Sisera, she pierced his head,
She split and struck through his temple.

At her feet he sank, he fell, he lay still;
At her feet he sank, he fell;
Where he sank, there he fell dead.

The mother of Sisera looked through the window,
And cried out through the lattice,
Why is his chariot so long in coming?
Why tarries the clatter of his chariots?'

Her wisest ladies answered her,
Yes, she answered herself,

Are they not finding and dividing the spoil:
To every man a girl or two;
For Sisera, plunder of dyed garments,
Plunder of garments embroidered and dyed,
Two pieces of dyed embroidery for the neck of the looter?'

Thus let all Your enemies perish, O Lord!
But let those who love Him be like the sun
When it comes out in full strength."
So the land had rest for forty years.

HANNAH

The Bible speaks to us of a pious and God-fearing man. His name was Elkana. He had two wives: Hannah and Penina. This was allowed at that time, but never a blessing for the family and even the children. Hannah was his favorite wife. She could not give birth because the Lord made her barren. Penina, her rival, lavished mortifications on her. She laughed at her; she insulted her; she was constantly mocked by her, because the Lord blessed her with several children, while Hannah was barren. This mockery went on for years.

No longer able to bear the intrigues of Penina, nor the reproach of sterility, Hannah burst into tears at the feet of the Lord. She only cried without eating in the presence of her God, rich in goodness and mercy.

During a fervent prayer, embellished with streams of sincere tears, she made a vow to the Lord saying: If you deign to look at the affliction of your servant, if you remember me and do not forget me your servant, and if you give your servant a son, I will consecrate him to you for the rest of his life.

O infinite compassion! During the same year, the Lord blessed the womb of Hannah who became pregnant and bore a son. This little boy, whom she named Samuel, became Israel's greatest and most faithful judge.

As the Lord testified his faithfulness to her, in return she testified her faithfulness and gratitude to the Holy One of Israel, the Supreme God, and did as she promised: Hannah lent Samuel to the Lord.

Not having been satisfied with her promise kept and her acts of gratitude before the perfection of God's love, compassion and faithfulness, she presented this song which bursts from her heart and filled her whole being.

SONG OF HANNAH: 1 SAMUEL 2:1-10

My heart rejoices in the Lord;
My horn is exalted in the Lord.
I smile at my enemies,
Because I rejoice in Your salvation.

No one is holy like the Lord,
For there is none besides You,
Nor is there any rock like our God.

Talk no more so very proudly;
Let no arrogance come from your mouth,
For the Lord is the God of knowledge;
And by Him actions are weighed.

The bows of the mighty men are broken,
And those who stumbled are girded with strength.

Those who were full have hired themselves out for bread,
And the hungry have ceased to hunger.
Even the barren has borne seven,
And she who has many children has become feeble.

The Lord kills and makes alive;
He brings down to the grave and brings up.

The Lord makes poor and makes rich;
He brings low and lifts up.

He raises the poor from the dust
And lifts the beggar from the ash heap,
To set them among princes
And make them inherit the throne of glory.

For the pillars of the earth are the Lord's,
And He has set the world upon them.
He will guard the feet of His saints,
But the wicked shall be silent in darkness.

For by strength no man shall prevail.
The adversaries of the Lord shall be broken in pieces;
From heaven He will thunder against them.
The Lord will judge the ends of the earth.

He will give strength to His king,
And exalt the horn of His anointed.

MARY, MOTHER OF JESUS

The virgin Mary was the most blessed among women, by the grace alone of being the mother of Jesus, who, being God himself, took the form of flesh or human form in her womb to come and save those who were lost; the rich and the poor, the learned and the ignorant, the strong and the weak. She received a visit from the angel Gabriel who said to her:" I greet you, you who have received a grace".

Mary began to be troubled. For such a visit, such a greeting was beyond his comprehension. It was really a real nightmare for her. And, the angel to continue: "You will become pregnant and you will give birth to a son, he will be great and will be called Son of the Most High and the Lord-God will give him the throne of David, his father. He will reign over the house of Jacob forever and his reign will have no end". (Luke 1:32-33)

Mary was a virgin of great faith. But, the mystery of the visit of the angel Gabriel and his message gave her a nightmare which had rightly paralyzed or limited her faith and caused her to ask this question: "How could it be, since I am virgin". The angel replied that "She would conceive by the power of the Spirit of God"." This is why", continues the angel: "The holy Child who will be born of you will be called Son of God". **(Luke 1:35)** It was then that the doors of her faith were opened and the light of the Holy Spirit illumined his heart. She now accepted with firmer faith and unprecedented humility the honor and the grace that God was mysteriously about to bestow upon her. The angel further informed her that her relative, Elizabeth, will also bear a son. Another joy was added to her already overflowing joy.

In no time, Mary hastened to go to Elizabeth's house, certainly to tell her this double and joyous news. Arriving there, she greeted Elizabeth who felt her child quiver in her womb. Filled with the Holy Spirit, she cried out with a loud voice: blessed are you among women, and blessed is the fruit of thy womb.

Grateful for the special honor God that "The mother of my Lord comes to me? For behold, as soon as the voice of your greeting struck my ear, the child leaped for joy in my bosom. Blessed is she who believed, because the things spoken to her from the Lord will come to pass".

Mary, considering the undeserved and unmeritorious grace which the living God has given her, glorified his holy name with a song which emptied all the content of her heart at his feet:

SONG OF MARY LUKE 1: 46-55

My soul magnifies the Lord,
And my spirit has rejoiced in God my Savior.
For He has regarded the lowly state of His maidservant;

For behold, henceforth all generations will call me blessed;
For He who is mighty has done great things for me,
And holy is His name.
And His mercy is on those who fear Him
From generation to generation

He has shown strength with His arm;
He has scattered the proud in the imagination of their hearts

He has put down the mighty from their thrones,
And exalted the lowly.

He has filled the hungry with good things,
And the rich He has sent away empty.

He has helped His servant Israel,
In remembrance of His mercy,

As He spoke to our fathers,
To Abraham and to his seed forever.

ZECHARIAH

Zechariah was a priest in Judea. His wife was called Elizabeth. Both feared the Lord and obeyed his commandments and judgments impeccably. They had no children because the Lord made Elizabeth barren. They were both advanced in age. While Zechariah was faithfully carrying out his task as priest in the temple, the angel Gabriel appeared to him and stood at the right of the altar of incense, the place where the priests presented their sacrifices to the Lord. Zechariah was disturbed on seeing him and fear seized him. But the angel assured him: "Do not be afraid Zechariah. Because your prayer has been answered. Your wife Elizabeth, who is old and barren, will bear you a son and you will name him John. He will be a source of joy and gladness for you, and many will rejoice at his birth. For he will be great before God and he will be filled with the Holy Spirit from his mother's womb. He will turn many of the sons of Israel back to the Lord their God; he will walk before God with the spirit and power of Elijah to bring back the rebels to the wisdom of the righteous in order to prepare a willing people": Zechariah replied to the angel: "By what shall I recognize him?" Because I am old and my woman is advanced in age. Since Zechariah doubted, the angel answered him: "I am Gabriel, I stand before God. I have been sent to speak to you and to announce this good news to you. And behold, you will be dumb, you will not be able to speak until the day when these things come to pass, because you did not believe my words which will come to pass in their time". Immediately after the angel's sentence, he became dumb, and when it was time for her bedtime, she would give birth to her child. Her neighbors and relatives, who heard, that the Lord had shown mercy to her, rejoiced with her. On the eighth day they came to circumcise the child, and they called him Zechariah, his father's name. But, Elizabeth spoke up and said no; he will be called John. Everyone was surprised. Because according to custom in Israel, the child should bear the name of his father or one of his parents. They asked Zechariah to name the child. Zechariah wrote: "John is his name". All were amazed.

At the same instant, his mouth opened; his tongue loosens and he speaks. He glorified and blessed the name of God. Fear seized all the inhabitants of the surrounding area.

Moved by the Holy Spirit and with a heart filled with gratitude, Zechariah exalted the Lord in this song of glory:

SONG OF ZECHARIAH LUKE 1:67-79

Praise be to the Lord, the God of Israel,
Because he has come to his people and redeemed them.

He has raised up a horn of salvation for us
In the house of his servant David
(as he said through his holy prophets of long ago),
Salvation from our enemies
And from the hand of all who hate us
To show mercy to our ancestors
And to remember his holy covenant,
The oath he swore to our father Abraham:

To rescue us from the hand of our enemies,
And to enable us to serve him without fear
In holiness and righteousness before him all our days.

And you, my child, will be called a prophet of the Most High;
For you will go on before the Lord to prepare the way for him,
To give his people the knowledge of salvation
Through the forgiveness of their sins,

Because of the tender mercy of our God,
By which the rising sun will come to us from heaven

To shine on those living in darkness
And in the shadow of death,
To guide our feet into the path of peace."

DAVID

David, which means beloved, was the youngest of the eight sons of Isaiah, also called Jesse. 1 Samuel 16:10-11; 17:12-14. His mother was very pious and is mentioned with tenderness and a feeling of piety in Psalms 86:16 and 116:16. Like our savior, he was born and raised in Bethlehem in Judea, but not at the same time. For David lived 113 years before our Savior was born. Since Jesus is a human descendant of David, biblical language called him son of David. (**Matthew 1:1**)

At a very young age, he was entrusted with the care of his father's sheep. Being brought up in godliness and in all the wisdom of God, the outdoors was a favorable opportunity to be in constant relationship with his divine Master.

Fiery, intrepid, and having on him the Spirit of God, he crushed lions and bears who came to attack his sheep. **1 Samuel 16:11; 17:34-36.** He was blessed with remarkable gifts of music, and was recognized as Israel's most talented musician. He was a composer and singer at the same time. When the Lord had rejected King Saul, he dispatched the prophet Samuel to Bethlehem and commanded him to anoint David to succeed him, but without open proclamation to avoid reprisals from Saul and his subjects.

After that, Saul lost the protection of God, was haunted by an evil spirit which subjected him to melancholy and fits of insanity. His servants advised him to employ a harpist whose music would calm his restlessness. As David was recognized by the greatest number as an excellent musician and a valiant young man, he was recommended to the king, who employed him without the slightest objection. Finally, his music appeased the madness of the king and his character pleased him too. Thus, he asked Jesse, David's father to leave him at the royal court and made him one of his squires (**1 Samuel 16:16-23; 2 Samuel 18:15**). Since he was responsible for carrying the king's shield. He accompanied him wherever he went. David who was very curious, learned about everything: the war, the monarchy, eminent men, friends of the king, the good and the bad side of the king's court.

David was not satisfied with the honor of being employed by the king, to forget his sheep. When David noticed that the evil spirit left the king, he asked him to let him go and help his father with the sheep. This request was granted, but his brothers: Eliab, Abimab, and Shammah remained with the king.

While he was away, the Philistines declared war on Judah and encamped at Soco, a city in Judah. As prompted by the providence of God, Jesse sent David, uninformed of the war, to bring provision to his brethren and inquire after them. Meanwhile, the armies of the Philistines were backed by the mighty Goliath who seemed able to shake the whole army of Israel. He was described by the Bible as follows: he had a height of six cubits and an ampan. The mathematical information leads us to this calculation: a cubit is equal to two ampans, plus one ampan. Two ampans are equal to 55 centimeters.

So Goliath had a height of (55x6)+ 27.5)= 357.5 cm; one foot equals 30.48 cm; dividing 357.5 by 30.48 (357.5: 30.48), it gives 10 feet 83 centimeters which is twice the normal height of a human being, more than twice the height of David who looked like a bird in his presence. That is why he was even called a giant. Not only did he have a height that inspired terror, his strength was indomitable. The description of his armor showed his strength. He had on his head a brazen helmet. He wore a scaled cuirass weighing five thousand shekels of brass; he had brazen armor on his legs and a brazen javelin between his shoulders; the weight of his spear was like a weaver's beam, and the spear weighed six hundred shekels of iron he imposed himself and presented this challenge to Israel: "Choose a man who comes down against me! If he can defeat me and kill me, we will be subject to you, but if I defeat him and let me kill him, you will be subject to us and you will serve us".

Confident in his indomitable strength, the fire of his pride ignited: "I challenge Israel this day! Give me a man and we'll fight together". Hearing these words, King Saul, his mighty army and all Israel were terrified and seized with great fear. It was then that David arrived. While he greeted his brothers, Goliath approached and held these same words. David heard him. Indignant, he exclaimed: "Who is this Philistine, this uncircumcised, to insult the army of the Lord?" His older brother, Eliab, accused him of being proud and presumptuous. He turned away from him and repeated the same question. Saul's allies heard David's words. They brought him back to King Saul who sent for him. Arrived near the king, the incredible David said to Saul: "Let no one be discouraged because of the Philistine: your servant will go and fight with him". Saul was smiling, of course, saying to David: "You cannot fight this Philistine, because you are a child, and Goliath is a man of war from his youth".

David boosted Saul's confidence with these words: "Your servant was tending his father's sheep; when a lion or a bear came to take one of the herd, I ran after him; I hit him and killed him. This is how your servant protected his father's sheep". David added: "The LORD who delivered me from the wolves and the bears, will also deliver me from the hand of Goliath". Convinced, Saul said to David: "Go, and may the LORD be with you". Now Saul ordered David to be dressed in military clothes. He put on his head a helmet of bronze, and clothed it with a breastplate. David girded his sword over his clothes, and wanted to walk, for he had not yet tried. But David, who was new to these military tactics, said to Saul:" I cannot walk in this armor, I am not accustomed to it", and he got rid of it. His only equipment was a stick, a shepherd's game bag, with five polished stones, which he put in his shepherd's satchel and in his pocket and a sling. He felt completely relieved. Then, he took his sling and advanced towards the Philistine who said to him: "Am I a dog, for you to come to me with sticks? Come to me, I will give your flesh to the birds of the sky and the beasts of the field". David answered him, "You will come against me with sword, spear, and javelin; and I come against you in the name of the LORD of hosts, of the God of the army of Israel whom you have insulted. I will fight with you and I will be victorious. And all the earth will know that Israel has a God. And all this multitude will know that it is neither by sword nor by spear that the Lord saves. For the victory belongs to the Lord".

David took a stone, placed it in his sling and threw it at the Philistine. The stone dug into his forehead and he fell face down. So the Lord granted victory and delivered Israel from the mighty hands of Goliath. Then the Lord delivered David from three attempts by Saul:

1) Although David served Saul with bravery and faithfulness, he was jealous of his exploits, and tried to kill him three times.
2) He begged Jonathan, his son and all his other servants to kill him. Jonathan, who was a loyal friend to David, informed him of this and warned him to be on his guard.
3) Immediately after a second victory that David won over the Philistines, instead of rewarding him and celebrating with him, his heart was swollen with jealousy.

Then the evil spirit from the Lord was upon Saul who was sitting in his house with his spear in his hand. Again David served Saul, playing the harp to drive out his evil spirit. Meanwhile, jealousy was so intense in his heart that he threw his spear to cut David. He escaped and fled.

Saul sent people to David's house to guard him and put him to death. Michal, daughter of Saul and wife of David informed him of this and made him escape through the window.

David realized that Saul was trying to kill him at all costs. In his despair, he took refuge in the country of the Philistines with six hundred men, their wives and their children. They went to Achish, king of Gath, land of the Philistines. He asked them for a place to stay, and the king gave him Tsiklkag.

David won several victories for Achish, which aroused in him a great affection for David. But, the Philistines who distrusted him, asked King Achish to send him back. The king informed him of this regrettable decision. David was saddened. When he returned from his meeting with the king, it was found that the Amélicites had made an invasion at Tsiklag, taking the women and all those who were there, young and old, prisoners. But the Lord did not permit them to do them any harm, because of David, his beloved. For the captives were his two wives and his servants.

His servants, worn down with sorrow and bitterness, wanted his life for their wives and their daughters and their sons. He was weak from crying. In his weakness he turned to his God and asked him: Shall I pursue this troop? And the LORD answered him, Go on. That's all David wanted to hear from his God who speaks and the thing happens. David, whose faith in his God is never tainted, pursued his invaders with six hundred men. Along the way, two hundred of them were too tired to continue. They stopped, and David continued with the remaining four hundred. The Lord sent him one of those who assisted him in the invasion of Tsiklag. We can guess that they were members of the army of the Lord. This man led David to his invaders.

On arriving, he found the Amelites scattered about the country, eating, drinking, and dancing, rejoicing in the great booty they had removed. David surprised them, beat them and saved all that the Amelicites were taken from him. He lacked no one, neither small nor great, neither sons nor daughters, nor anything that was taken from him. On that day the Lord granted David unprecedented victory and deliverance. After rejoicing in still greater victories and deliverances, he has now taken time to review all the victories and deliverances which the Lord has bestowed on him in return for the bloody hand of all his enemies, especially the hand of Saul, David composed this song to place at the feet of the incredibly faithful and almighty God, his cup of his eternal gratitude.

SONG OF DAVID 2 SAMUEL 22:1-51

The Lord is my rock and my fortress and my deliverer;
The God of my strength, in whom I will trust;
My shield and the horn of my salvation,
My stronghold and my refuge;

My Savior, You save me from violence.
I will call upon the Lord, who is worthy to be praised;
So shall I be saved from my enemies.
When the waves of death surrounded me,
The floods of ungodliness [b]made me afraid.
The sorrows of Sheol surrounded me;
The snares of death confronted me.
 In my distress I called upon the Lord,

And cried out to my God;
He heard my voice from His temple,
And my cry entered His ears.
Then the earth shook and trembled;
The foundations of heaven quaked and were shaken,
Because He was angry.

 Smoke went up from His nostrils,
And devouring fire from His mouth;
Coals were kindled by it.
He bowed the heavens also, and came down
With darkness under His feet.
 He rode upon a cherub, and flew;
And He was seen upon the wings of the wind.
 He made darkness canopies around Him,
Dark waters and thick clouds of the skies.
 From the brightness before Him
Coals of fire were kindled.

The Lord thundered from heaven,
And the Most High uttered His voice.
He sent out arrows and scattered them;
Lightning bolts, and He vanquished them.
Then the channels of the sea were seen,
The foundations of the world were uncovered,
At the rebuke of the Lord,
At the blast of the breath of His nostrils.

He sent from above, He took me,
He drew me out of many waters.
He delivered me from my strong enemy,
From those who hated me;
For they were too strong for me.
They confronted me in the day of my calamity,
But the Lord was my support.
He also brought me out into a broad place;
He delivered me because He delighted in me.

The Lord rewarded me according to my righteousness;
According to the cleanness of my hands
He has recompensed me.
For I have kept the ways of the Lord,
And have not wickedly departed from my God.
For all His judgments were before me;
And as for His statutes, I did not depart from them.
 I was also blameless before Him,
And I kept myself from my iniquity.
Therefore the Lord has recompensed me according to my righteousness,
According to my cleanness in His eyes.

With the merciful You will show Yourself merciful;
With a blameless man You will show Yourself blameless;
With the pure You will show Yourself pure;
And with the devious You will show Yourself shrewd.
You will save the humble people;
But Your eyes are on the haughty, that You may bring them down.

For You are my lamp, O Lord;
The Lord shall enlighten my darkness.
For by You I can run against a troop;
By my God I can leap over a wall.
As for God, His way is perfect;
The word of the Lord is proven;
He is a shield to all who trust in Him.

For who is God, except the Lord?
And who is a rock, except our God?
God is my strength and power,
And He makes my way perfect.
He makes my feet like the feet of deer,
And sets me on my high places.
He teaches my hands to make war,
So that my arms can bend a bow of bronze.

You have also given me the shield of Your salvation;
Your gentleness has made me great.
You enlarged my path under me;
So my feet did not slip.

I have pursued my enemies and destroyed them;
Neither did I turn back again till they were destroyed.
And I have destroyed them and wounded them,
So that they could not rise;
They have fallen under my feet.
For You have armed me with strength for the battle;
You have subdued under me those who rose against me.
You have also given me the necks of my enemies,
So that I destroyed those who hated me.
They looked, but there was none to save;
Even to the Lord, but He did not answer them.
Then I beat them as fine as the dust of the earth;
I trod them like dirt in the streets,
And I spread them out.

You have also delivered me from the strivings of my people;
You have kept me as the head of the nations.
A people I have not known shall serve me.
The foreigners submit to me;
As soon as they hear, they obey me.
The foreigners fade away,
And come frightened from their hideouts.

The Lord lives!
Blessed be my Rock!
Let God be exalted,
The Rock of my salvation!
It is God who avenges me,
And subdues the peoples under me;
He delivers me from my enemies.
You also lift me up above those who rise against me;
You have delivered me from the violent man.
Therefore I will give thanks to You, O Lord, among the Gentiles,
And sing praises to Your name.

He is the tower of salvation to His king,
And shows mercy to His anointed,
To David and his descendants forevermore."

MORALES

You have been, a while ago, informed of the origin and growth of my life in Christ, where I have already recounted the memorable marvels which the Lord has wrought in my life, and my supplications to the Most High to grant me the grace to add my song to those of his holy servants: Moses, Deborah, Hannah, Mary, Zechariah, and David. He granted my prayer. Now, sing with me, this song of perfect gratitude, addressed to this Eternal God, this adorable Redeemer; this God who by his omniscience, his omnipotence and his omnipresence, tore the net of the fowler and saved me by the power of his right hand.

SONG OF MORALES

Where did I find myself?
And where have you placed me,
King of nations, King of the ages?

You, whose decision is made,
And blessings, final.
Who can add or subtract to your blessings,
God of gods?

All your decisions are right,
And your deeds are perfect
Where did I find myself?
And where have you placed me,
King of Glory, infinite Wisdom?

In the company of my savior Jesus -Christ?
Sitting with Moses, Deborah, Hannah,
Mary, Zechariah, and David?
Mystery of mysteries!

From the dust, you lifted me up.
Descendant of a little camper without hope,
I was lost in the forest.
You looked for me.

You found me in the middle of the woods
You raised me up, you raised me up,
You raised me up beyond what
I would have ever thought and dreamed.

Have I become an insane dreamer?
No, I'm not dreaming;
No, I'm not losing my common sense!
It Is just plain truth.

You have already revealed yourself
To my predecessors.
They believed and saw your glory.
They told me of your marvels;

They instructed me of your wonders.
They taught me that your compassions lean
Towards the oppressed;
That by the power of your right hand.

You have dethroned invincible kings.
You broke the bow of Argon, fearsome king of Bashan,
And of Sihon, mighty king of the Amoreans.
Who is and will ever be like you on earth, as it is in heaven?

Because you are omnipotent
You have set a table in front
Of your servants'adversaries.
They have set up ambushes to surprise your saints.

They sent charcals and ostriches to devour them.
Your right hand surprised them in all their might,
And you delivered your holy ones.
We are the apple of your eyes,

Who can touch us?
Who can destroy us?
You live forever, oh my God,
And your power cannot ever be compared.

I have heard, I have seen,
And I have testified that you are the only true God.
You have no beginning, no end.
You lived by yourself before the beginning of time.

You are God!
You are the creator of time,
Heaven and earth!
That all that exists,
Humbles himself before you

To sing in unison: REAL! REAL!
You are the only true God!
We certify and we confess
That there is no other god but YOU!

You are worthy of our worship!
You are worthy of our love!
You are worthy of our trust!
You are worthy of our praise!
And may you live forever! Amen! Amen! Amen!

www.ingramcontent.com/pod-product-compliance
Lightning Source LLC
Chambersburg PA
CBHW071016120626
46546CB00003B/1120

* 9 7 8 1 9 6 3 9 1 7 0 3 1 *